Five Thousand Years of Theatre

Five Thousand Years —of Theatre——————

Jack Mitchley
Peter Spalding

Drawings by Anthony Kinsey

Holmes & Meier Publishers
New York

First published in the United States of America 1982 by
Holmes & Meier Publishers, Inc.
30 Irving Place, New York, N.Y. 10003

Library of Congress Cataloging in Publication Data

Mitchley, Jack.
   5,000 years of the theatre.

   Bibliography: p.
   Includes index.
   1. Theater—History.   I. Spalding, Peter.
II. Title.   III. Title: Five thousand years of the theatre.
PN2101.M57   792′.09   81–20156
ISBN 0–8419–0783–8   AACR2

Printed in Great Britain

Contents

Preface 7

Introduction 10

1 Arts of Making — Arts of Doing 11

THE ESSENCE OF THEATRE; ARTS AND AUDIENCE; FORM AND MEDIA; ARTS AS MAGIC

2 Origins and Survivals 18

SURVIVING PRIMITIVE ART; ANIMALS IN RITUAL; SEASONAL FESTIVALS; PATTERNS OF RITUAL

3 Early Religious Festivals: the West 25

EGYPT; THE GREEKS; THE ROMANS

4 Early Religious Festivals: the East 38

INDIA; INDONESIA; JAPAN; CHINA

FIRST INTERLUDE 47

5 Religious Drama in Medieval Europe 49

THE JESTER; THE TROPE; TYPES OF PLAY; THE MANSION; THE MEDIEVAL ROUND; SECULARIZATION AND THE RISE OF PROFESSIONALISM; PAGEANT CARTS; THE GUILDMAN PLAYER; POLITICS AND THE PLAYER

SECOND INTERLUDE 61

6 The Shape of the Stage 62

THE BOOTH; PHYLAX; COMMEDIA DELL'ARTE; PEKIN OPERA

7 The Elizabethan Playhouse 71

GAMESHOUSES; THE THEATRE: 1756; THE DEVELOPED BOOTH: THE ELIZABETHAN PLAYHOUSE; THE ACTORS; THE MASQUE; THE GREAT DESIGNER: INIGO JONES; THE 'PRIVATE' THEATRES

8 A Roof over their Heads 84

ITALIAN STYLE; FRENCH STYLE; ENGLISH STYLE: RESTORATION; ENGLISH STYLE: GEORGIAN

9 The Nineteenth Century 99

SCENIC ILLUSION AND DISILLUSION; STAGE LIGHTING; 'AN ACTOR'S LIFE FOR ME' — THE TOURING THEATRES OF THE NINETEENTH CENTURY

THIRD INTERLUDE 109

10 Nineteenth-century Anti-illusion 110

ADOLPH APPIA; GORDON CRAIG; REALISM; REALISM: EUROPE AND THE USA; TWENTIETH-CENTURY DEVELOPMENTS

11 The Twentieth Century 119

NEW APPROACHES TO SHAKESPEARE; DIRECTOR'S THEATRE; STRATFORD, ONTARIO; THEATRE-IN-THE-ROUND; ADAPTABLE THEATRE

POSTCRIPT 131
Bibliography 133
Index 135

Preface

Why this book when there are many large and beautifully illustrated histories of theatre? To this we have two answers. The first is that our book, by a process of compression, both of narrative and illustration, is intended to provide both student and general reader with a survey of world theatre in a light, handy and moderately priced form.

Secondly, despite our compression, we can claim to offer the reader more than a mere list of historical facts. We ourselves have always been deeply curious as to why theatre buildings and acting styles have shown such radical differences throughout their history—and also such radical similarities! We do not claim to know the answer to every problem, but we do suggest that the most important clues will always be found either in the study of the ritual origins of theatre, on the one hand, or in the commercial practices of the professional entertainer on the other.

In this, and throughout our work, our principal guide has been Dr Richard Southern, whose seminal work *Seven Ages of Theatre* is our key source.

We must also acknowledge our gratitude to Tony Kinsey for his simple and ingenious illustrations and Thelma Nye for her encouragement, patience and sympathetic editing.

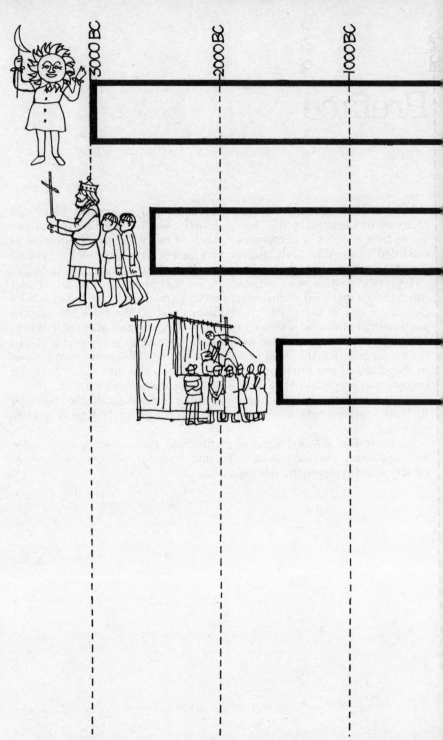

Histogram designed to show the continuing existence of the costumed actor with no permanent stage or auditorium. Note also the long history of the booth stage as compared with the picture-frame/proscenium type of the last 150 years

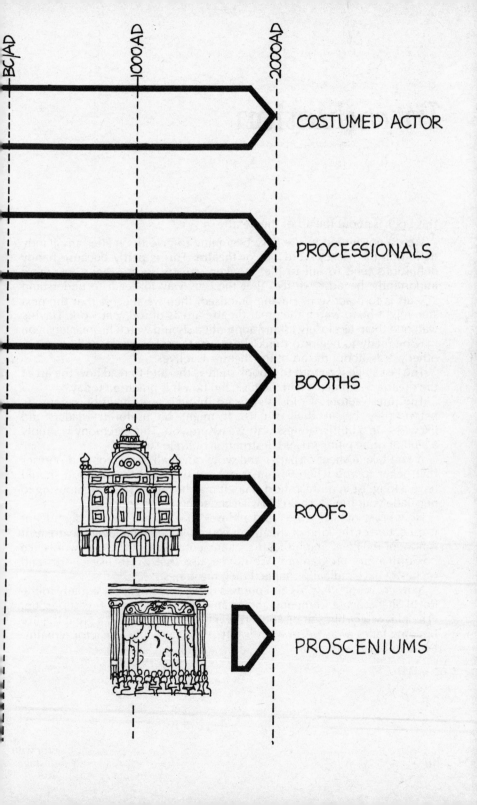

BC/AD   1000AD   2000AD

COSTUMED ACTOR

PROCESSIONALS

BOOTHS

ROOFS

PROSCENIUMS

Introduction

This book is about the art of the theatre.

We do not intend at the very beginning to give the reader any handy definition of the key words **art** or **theatre**. This is partly because handy definitions tend to fail to please when you try to use them but, more importantly, because we feel that the only way to begin to understand any art is to practise it. Having practised, then we suggest that the next step might be to watch the great theatre artists of today at work. Having watched them as closely as any apprentice should watch his masters, you may be ready to begin to think about what you have seen and heard. In other words, about the art of the theatre as it lives.

The last stage is to turn to a book such as this and to read how the art of the theatre was practised in the past and how it is practised today.

The priest-actors of old used to go through a purification ceremony before they began their rituals. It might be useful if readers did likewise—in a quite painless way, we assure you. This ceremony is simply a kind of ritual piling up and destruction of irrelevancies.

If you take a sheet of paper and write down all the words and phrases that occur to you when you hear or read the word theatre, you should have a long list in quite a short time. It may be interesting and amusing to persuade your friends to do likewise and to compare your lists.

Now cross out all words and phrases that do not remain significant irrespective of the kind of theatre in your mind, eg your local theatre as it is now, or the great amphitheatres of ancient Greece. (There go words like box-office and programme! We notice also that words like chorus and orchestra have radically changed their meanings.)

Now cross out all words and phrases that could not apply equally to the Royal Shakespeare Company and to an improvising street theatre-group. (The playwright himself disappears, even the greatest, and a great theatre building fades away.) And what is left? Well, certainly the actor remains. So let us begin with him.

1
Arts of Making
—Arts of Doing————

The actors' art is older than the theatres of ancient Greece. It is older than the plays written by the priests of ancient Egypt. Indeed, it can exist without a theatre building and even without a play, in the usual sense of the word.

This art is not only very old but spread throughout the whole world, so that there is hardly a country which has never had native theatre of some kind or other. Yet the picture can appear confusing and contradictory. Almost anything that we could say about the actor and his art in one place at one time may appear no longer to be true as time and circumstances change.

The place of the actor within his own society has changed. He has been hailed as a king, venerated as a priest, even worshipped as a god; but he has also been despised as a vagabond and imprisoned as a felon, pampered as an entertaining pet and, of late by the English, has been dubbed a knight and even elevated to the House of Lords.

In many countries, including our own, theatre is mostly a commercial enterprise with only the most tenuous links with religion. In others, the theatre is virtually inseparable from religion. So an audience from Bali transported to Broadway, while its members might have pleasure in what they see and hear, might find it very difficult to understand.

Even within theatres that at first sight might seem at least roughly similar, there is tremendous variety of techniques. Some actors never speak; others speak but are not seen to move. Some actors speak only what is written down; others always improvise their lines. Some wear elaborate costumes, masks or mask-like make-up; others appear in ordinary dress. Some deliberately call attention to their bravura acting skills; others like to pretend they are not acting at all.

In the face of the length of history and the cultural diversity of the art of theatre, how can we begin to describe it in so short a book? Are there really behind all these differences some things in common, some truths that held in the Athens of Aeschylus and still hold in the London of Ayckbourn? Or can something be said of the Japanese Noh play that is also true of political street theatre in Birmingham? Obviously we believe so, or we would not be writing this book. We also believe that we can arrive at the essence of theatre by a process of elimination.

THE ESSENCE OF THEATRE

A very great writer on these matters, Richard Southern, in his book *The Seven Ages of Theatre*, suggests that the essence of theatre resides in two basic elements, contained within a third. These are the actor, the costumed player, and his audience together in a shared space. This statement, like all fundamental truths, may appear a little obvious, but once we begin to consider the infinite varieties of costume for the player and the psychological geometry of the space in which he works, we may well discover surprising things.

Let us now consider the costumed player in relation to other artists and in relation to the lofty concept of art. Some questions arise. For instance, does Mr Southern mean that a great actor, costumed as Hamlet on the stage at Stratford-on-Avon itself, is engaged in precisely the same activity as our own Uncle Jim dressed in a top hat and baggy trousers, juggling oranges at a children's party? Yes. But can this activity be described in both instances as art? Yes. Although we must remember that to categorize any activity as art does not imply a judgement of quality. (Recently one critic said, 'Anything is art, if an artist says it is art', and another critic replied, 'Yes, but there is still good art and bad art'.)

Should we then try to define the term 'art'? No. We could go through another sieving process starting from the word 'art' itself, but it would take a very long time. Let us instead admit that we are quite capable of recognizing the various arts as we experience them, whether we are able to define them or not.

ART AND AUDIENCE

When we consider all the arts we notice similarities and differences between them. One fairly obvious similarity is that most (if not all) artists seem to need an audience of some sort. Not necessarily for themselves but for their art or the product of their art. This audience may be approached directly as by performers or indirectly by creative artists working through the performers. (Examples here are the actor, musician or dancer in the first instance and the playwright, composer or choreographer in the second.)

There is another kind of artist who does not seem to approach or reach out to an audience. He seems to be quite content to make something and then not even bother to display it. Even if he does display it he does not need to be present while his work of art is in front of its audience. These are the *making* artists—the painters, sculptors and writers.

To say that all works of art contain a message is to over-simplify and to suggest that art exists merely to serve education, advertisement or propaganda. Yet *something* other than the work of art itself appears to pass from artist to audience. Southern uses the term address. He says that 'any work of art is an address (in some form) by an individual to a number of people.'

FORM AND MEDIA

The concept of form in art is complex, but for our present purpose we need consider only two aspects of it. First, we can say that it is by recognition of form that we recognize the experience of art. We have learned to know the symphony within the art-form of music, for instance, or the novel within literature, and so on. Some authorities speak of received form in this context. Certainly if we find it difficult to recognize the form we tend to reject the work of art. (We say something like—'A pile of bricks is not art'.)

Secondly, the form itself depends upon the media used (ie, the raw materials and tools). The sculptor may need stone and chisels, etc. The writer, paper and a typewriter. By recognizing the materials and processes involved, we recognize not only the general experience of art, but can begin to classify the various works of art according to the medium used.

Making and doing

The very limitations of the media account for differences between the arts of making and doing. Until the invention of film, television and other recording devices, the performers, the 'doing' artists, had to be physically present before the eyes and ears of their audiences. The actor, the dancer, the singer, the instrumentalist, etc, use their own physical equipment as raw material and work on it with their skills. Each performance is unique (and, to quote Beckett, given 'astride a grave').

Mention of recording devices must not blind us to the fact that whatever is on the tape or disc is *not* the performance. Performance cannot happen until there is an audience—and no good theatre artist, though he exploits recording devices, would ever play to anything that was not alive, if he had free choice.

One way to appreciate the difference between the arts of making and of doing is to practise them. If you were called upon, as students sometimes are, to make a mask for your own use in a performance, you would experience not only the physical feel of the tools and raw materials, but certain emotions as well. The tutor would be well aware of this; as well as instructing the students in the skills required, he might be aiming to educate them through their emotional involvement. For instance the choice of style for the mask may be left to them, so that they experience the first agony of any artist—'What shall I make?'. After a few tentative experiments with paint brush or scissors an idea may begin, however slowly, to emerge. As we have said, the *form* of the work of art is conditioned by its medium. Once the ideas begin to 'catch', the students begin to become involved, sometimes quite excited by the act of 'making'.

This kind of experience is familiar to most of us. Perhaps we did this sort of thing when we were young children and have never done it since, more's the pity!

Now it does not seem to matter what kind of art is under consideration. The process, as seen from inside by the artist, seems to be remarkably similar whether the artist is performer or maker. The feelings are alike and the same sort of phrases are used to discuss them by painters, composers, writers, actors, musicians, etc. Furthermore, both student beginners and experienced masters of the art seem to experience a similar emotional pattern.

To return to the mask-making exercise, at first the students may all be in different emotional states—some eager, some bored, some timid or confident, co-operative or resentful. The tutor will not be worried by this. In fact he would be more worried if all his students did exactly what he told them without feeling or showing any emotion at all.

The most important thing in the making of any work of art is to build up emotional energy. The stimulus of working with colours and the general feeling of playing about begins to release the students' energy in a pleasurable way. After the making of the first masks, the experiment could end. It could end perhaps in failure, boredom, frustration for some or for most. It could end with reasonable success for most and a feeling of moderate satisfaction but with no strong desire to continue. This is what happens most of the time in most of our attempts to make or do a work of art. (That is a sad but true fact that any experienced artist will accept.) But if the experiment is really to succeed, then the mask makers will not want to stop. They will want to continue because what they are making is, in some way, a part of themselves, and furthermore a part of themselves which they wish to share with other people.

This sharing is what Southern means by the artist *addressing* a number of people. At this stage the people working become quieter, more absorbed, more concerned with getting every detail as right as it possibly can be. The flow of energy is now going from the makers into what they are making. When the energy-flow is complete then the object of art has been made. It may be shown. It *must* be shown.

It is at this point that the difference between maker and performer becomes crystal clear. The maker can now display his object, charged with energy, in a public place and he can walk away from it. It was a part of him, but is no longer so. The performer can not do this, because he is an essential part of what he makes and he cannot share or show his art without using himself to do it. Furthermore, an actor is *not* a performer until he faces an audience and begins to perform. (This would imply that many of us who spent hours and hours in *reading* the works of Shakespeare, may have been studying great literature but were not learning much about the art of theatre!)

In the practice of all arts, at the beginning of a new project there always occurs a period of self consciousness, awkwardness and indecision. Southern, in his book, refers to these feelings under the general heading of *nervousness*. This, strangely enough, is necessary to build up the energy which will flow from the maker into the work and from the work to the audience. Every actor has experienced stage fright, but this is an extreme form of nervousness which has become disabling. Every actor knows that the opposite of stage fright—an overweening self

Diagrammatic impression of the development of group or tribal dance/drama
activity through the emergence of expert leaders (a choir in Christian terms) and
on to organized performance of the priest/actor figure

2
Origins and Survivals

The main thesis of this book was stated at the end of the Introduction. It must now be our business to validate it and to elaborate upon it in the light of whatever evidence we can find.

Let us begin by testing our statement about primitive man as a general artist. The Magdalenian people, who lived many thousands of years ago in the early Stone Age, drew pictures on cave walls. At Trois Frères, in Southern France, there is a painting which depicts a personage who is like a man but with a horse's tail and a bison's head. He has the front legs of an animal, but appears to be playing what could be a bowed musical instrument. Furthermore his attitude suggests that he is dancing. He is preceded by two animals, one of which turns its head to look back at him. It may be tempting to seize upon this as evidence of primitive man as general practising artist. We could claim that this is a self portrait of a magician who was also a mask maker, musician and dancer. Of course we must avoid this temptation, but equally we can safely accept that this, and other paintings of this period, indicate that man was already an artist.

Most anthropologists would say that primitive man never practised art for its own sake. Invariably art had a very practical purpose—bringing about desired events or averting disaster, by means of the magic inherent in the process of making the work of art itself. Sometimes, as in the case of the ritual mask, the artefact itself retained its own magic.

When we contemplate a cave painting of men with bows and arrows preparing for a battle or for hunting, we note that many of these paintings are far from crude. They are the work of thoughtful, feeling adults. Primitive art is not inferior art; primitive drama is not inferior drama. The paintings have beauty to our eyes, although the concept of 'beauty' would be incomprehensible to the artists who made them. We may ask how far it is true that the paintings could have been just one part of a complete ritual involving speech, song, music and dance as well? We can never know for certain what happened 10,000 years ago, but if we examine those peoples who remained in a Stone Age culture until recent times we are led to believe that all the arts were used simultaneously to create the necessary emotional excitement for a successful hunt or battle.

In any case, one does not need to be an anthropologist to guess that what later became fixed as a ritual *could* arise naturally during the very act of preparation. To practice the handling of weapons for war or hunting, can lead naturally to the beginnings of dance; to grunt with effort, to chant in rhythm, to shout boastfully together is the beginning of song. Furthermore, if one is led in this exercise by a chieftain who calls upon beneficent spirits to assist in the enterprise, then ritual may become established. Such a ritual would contain within it reference to the tribal mythology, so at this point it may well be useful to consider the use made by the primitive artist, and later by the costumed player, of the art of storytelling. (This later became dignified with the title of 'literature' but let us for the present just think of it as storytelling.)

Time and again, we find the costumed player engaged in the enactment of myth. In social anthropology, the concept of myth is complex and controversial but it is safe to say that primitive man invented storytelling along with the other arts. Again the purpose was practical. He told stories to entertain people, to counteract the boredom of the winter nights, and he told stories to instruct the young, and to explain the universe to them. From telling a story to enacting it is a major step forward indeed, but it is a step regularly taken by children today, so it is safe to assume that primitive man did likewise and was author as well as painter, dancer and the rest.

SURVIVING PRIMITIVE ART

We shall now consider the use of all the arts by a tribe of Indians living in Brazil today. They are the Mehinacu who live under protection according to their own customs in a culture very similar to that of the Stone Age itself. The following description is based upon a television film made for the 'Disappearing World' series; it provides interesting examples of art being used to work magic. These Indians are animists. That is to say they act on the assumption that most things in nature, such as trees and roots, etc, are inhabited by spirits. The ceremonies that we see them prepare and perform are towards a very practical end. 'We have rituals for piqui spirits, to let them have their food', a spokesman says. 'If they do not have their food, they are sad. If we didn't feed the spirits there would not be any piqui'. 'Piqui' is the piqui nut which, with fish, is the staple diet of the tribe. The spirits are invited into the village and given a feast. If the spirits were not invited, then they would be angry, make the people ill, and eventually the people would die because the spirits would not allow the piqui nut to grow.

The entire ceremony is organised by the men. The women are allowed to participate at certain times only. Originally, it is said, the magic flutes used for calling the spirits were kept by the women. One of the ritual dance dramas depicts the women (impersonated gleefully by the men) failing to handle the flutes correctly and being unable to get the right sound out of them, so that the spirits are highly amused but do not come. This story is told and enacted to explain how it comes about that the flutes are kept in the Men's House, away from women. Each spirit has a name and a recognizable appearance but although they are ever present in the forest, they usually remain invisible. Therefore they have to be made visible if they are to take part in the ceremony.

At this point, we may remember that the distinguished producer Peter Brook in his book, *The Empty Space,* refers to what he calls Holy Theatre, that is to say, religious theatre in the widest sense of the word, as 'the theatre of the invisible made visible'.

The men construct masks and figures to be inhabited by the spirits. When the spirits do come to inhabit them they will be dangerous to ordinary people, including the people who made them, but they explain that the figures will not become live and dangerous until they are painted. 'Once it's painted,' the Mehinacu artist explains, 'it must be fed or it will be angry with us.' This is an example of art being seen as magic, so that magic can manifest itself through art. Once the painted constructions are made, they are taken into the forest by certain members of the tribe who have the task of animating them.

There is an interesting convention observed here, as in all similar ceremonies. If a member of the tribe goes into the forest to become a costumed player—a representative of spirits, then he *becomes* the spirit. This means that he ceases to exist as himself for the duration of the ritual. At the given hour, music is started and the people in the village begin to chant an invocation and out of the forest the spirits appear. Each particular spirit has its own appearance and character and is allocated a particular place in the sequence of performances. The rituals vary. Some spirits are playful, some terrifying and some are actually attacked and insulted by the women. Although the ceremonies have a very serious purpose, everybody expects them to be very enjoyable.

ANIMALS IN RITUAL

Can we claim that we have established a connection between primitive rituals such as these and more formal religious drama? And what connection have either with that which takes place in theatres of today? In the same way that the ruins of an ancient monastery may stand preserved in the middle of a council estate, so there are survivals in the arts —oddities that continue to exist and may be so old that even those who take part in them cannot tell you very much about their origins. If we study these survivals, we may find the connections we seek. For instance, if we take as a starting point the cave painting in France and presume for the moment that the man depicted who dressed himself up as an animal was indeed a magician, it would be interesting if we could find an example in the present time of a player whose costume was that of an animal. Setting aside our old friend the pantomime horse, who might be somewhat taken aback to find himself treated so seriously and to be regarded as being concerned with magic and ritual, we nevertheless find that some of his relations have been very deeply involved is such sinister goings on. Indeed, horses, dragons and the like constantly appear in rituals concerned with death and resurrection. The Chinese dragon that takes part in New Year ceremonies and has twice as many feet as there are people to get under his long coloured cloak, dances around and invites you to greet him. To shake hands with the dragon, the Chinese say, is to accept life for one more year, for good or evil. He is always accompanied by the beating of gongs and the sound of fireworks, to drive away lesser and evil spirits and he is welcomed with flowers.

In Bali, where all drama is religious, one of the most spectacular and ancient events is the fight between the Barong, a two-person dragon, of great beauty, presence and power, against the witch, Rangda. At first, Rangda defeats the Barong. The villagers are appalled and draw daggers to avenge their dragon but, as they advance upon the witch, she sends them into a mediumistic trance, so that their daggers are turned in their hands against themselves. (This is not necessarily simulated. The trance and subsequent wounds may be real.) The Barong returns yet, strangely enough, the play never ends with victory for one or the other. Rangda simply fades away when the play is stopped, usually by a Brahmin priest. It is said that the whole performance may symbolize the overcoming of devil worship by a more kindly religion from India. Others say that it admits a basic truth—that good and evil are co-existent and interdependent, and speak of Yang and Yin (see Chapter 4).

Christian mythology says that when the dragon lost his wings, he became a serpent. From being a power for good he became the devil. We in the West, and particularly in England, have our dragon. This is St. George's dragon and there is an ancient traditional play about him. It might be older than Christianity. Norwich museum possesses a very famous medieval dragon called 'Snap'. He was probably used in processional plays at Corpus Christi (see Chapter 5). There is also a very alarming object which can be described as follows: It is a black mask with a tall pointed headdress. On the headdress are white lines. White lines encircle the eyes. The point of the headdress is crowned with a bow or knot of hair. A red tongue hangs from the mouth. There are heavy grey eyebrows and a beard of hair. Great ears project on each side. When the mask is assumed by a man there spreads out from its neck a circle of black material some five feet in diameter stretching horizontally on a hoop at the level of the wearer's shoulders. From the hoop depends a sort of skirt also in black covering the wearer to the ground. From the front of this projects a small carved horse's head with a movable jaw and a mane and from the rear there is a tail of horse hair. This strange beast comes not from Bali nor from New Guinea, although both Balinese and New Guinea man might half recognize it. It belongs to the town of Padstow in Cornwall. At certain times of the year especially May Day it is brought out and led through the streets and dances at the command of its leader. It is known as the hobby-horse and at one time England had many of these animals. Strange rituals have also persisted around such commonplace agricultural implements as the plough.

SEASONAL FESTIVALS

Within living memory, it used to be the custom in Norfolk and elsewhere on the Monday following Twelfth Day, for the ploughmen to take a holiday and have their own special ceremony. This took the form of a procession, in which Fool's Plough, an ordinary plough decorated with ribbons, was dragged along by ploughmen dressed in clean white smocks decorated with ribbons. Sometimes they blacked their faces or wore masks. The procession was led by a man dressed as an old woman, carrying a collecting box. The explanation usually given for this custom is that it is a continuance, just for the fun of it, of a pre-Christian custom. It was believed that taking a plough away from the land it was used on, for a tour around the neighbouring hamlets, would lure evil spirits away from the fields and confuse them so that they would never find their way back again. This may sound aimless to the point of naivety, but the explanation has the authority of anthropologists, who state that this kind of ritual occurs throughout the world.

The Marshfield Mummers' Play also has many features suggesting an origin deep in the ritual past. A century ago there were still hundreds of these plays being performed in country districts. There were individual variations in dialogue and in the names of the characters, but the basic plot and the style of playing was remarkably similar. Marshfield is one of the very few survivors. Although we believe that the play as it survives is no older than the eighteenth century, being based on the script of *The Seven Champions of Christendom,* we suspect that mumming itself is of great antiquity. (Readers are referred to Sir E. E. Chambers' book about it.)

A visitor to Marshfield, in Gloucestershire, on Boxing Day morning who takes his place in the market place with the crowd at the appointed time, will hear the town band approaching followed by the Town Crier and the Seven Mummers. The Town Crier will ring his bell and will introduce them as 'The Famous Marshfield Mummers'—the old time paper boys. The strange description is justified in that the Mummers are dressed from head to foot in strips of paper, completely covering their faces and bodies. They can see through the paper strips, but no one in the audience could possibly recognize them. Some carry swords; one carries a doctor's bag, others, different attributes. The language is ritualized and begins with a request for space: 'Room! Room! A gallant room I say!' They form a circle, as the crowd makes way for them. Immediately the first character introduces himself by name and challenges another character to a duel. This is fought with swords, until one is slain, and the doctor is called upon to cure him. The play continues until all seven characters have introduced themselves and taken part in the story. Then the music plays, a collection is made for charity and the mummers move on to repeat the performance elsewhere in the town.

Just as the Padstow horse might remind us of a New Guinea mask, then the Marshfield Mummers' papers might remind us of the costume of African witchdoctors or, more accurately, of the members of a male secret society. It used to be said that members of the village Mummers were never very communicative about their art. Whether this was simply due to boredom at the oft repeated questions of curious people or had deeper reasons, we do not know. But they do say, in Marshfield, that whatever the weather has been like on Christmas Day, it always clears in time for the play on Boxing Day!

PATTERNS OF RITUAL

When we contemplate these survivals we can begin to see a pattern emerging. First of all we notice that all our examples seem to be concerned with a particular season of the year—sometimes, even, a special day. The dates chosen are either religious festivals or days such as Plough Monday which appear to have their origins in nature-worship. These were pagan and, in Europe, were either suppressed or prettified by the Christian authorities so that the serious sexual symbolism of the Hobby Horse was ignored as holiday buffoonery. Secondly the costume is of paramount importance and serves to obliterate the wearer so that he is seen in his symbolic role only. The costume itself is always bizarre and frequently intended to be terrifying. Thirdly, the dialogue is often in verse, always rhythmic and formally constructed—rather like a sort of liturgy. The manner of speech is not naturalistic but declamatory. There is a practical point here. Verse is easier to memorize, the more doggerel the easier, hence the success of so many doggerel mnemonics. Furthermore not only in the English Mumming plays but in other costume drama all over the world, the protagonists introduce themselves to the audience in a manner that implies that the audience should *already know their names*. Imagine the effect of being confronted at a rural festival in the primitive past by a larger than life figure that says 'I am your God!'

Finally, from Bali to Marshfield, there seems to be an element of ritual killing and resurrection, with the action frequently contained within a circle. There are practical reasons for this, but we must remember that the circle is symbolic of all recurring processes, of life and death, of seed-time and harvest and eternity itself. But as an antidote to over-solemnity let us remember that many of these ceremonies had lighter moments. (After all, the natural cheerfulness of people will keep breaking through.)

We have now ranged through nine thousand years of history and more or less circumnavigated the globe in search of the origins of the arts of theatre. What we have found tends to show that the art begins not in a building dedicated to the purpose, nor with a work of literature intended for performance, but with a ritual act. Such an act was magical in origin and later became religious. The men who undertake to lead this act always seem to need a costume in which to perform. Usually, but not invariably, they seem to need musical instruments and other properties. We must emphasize that, although some of these ceremonies had elements of terror in them and were always serious in purpose, there is no doubt whatever that the people who originated them also took great pleasure from taking part in them. This comes out very clearly in the film of the Brazilian ritual described above, particularly in the sequence where the women attack and humiliate the visiting spirits. By the end of this everybody is helpless with laughter and the genuine inter-sexual rivalry which could be a source of danger to the community has been channelled and so made harmless.

This reminds us that one function of theatre has always been entertainment. If the performance is not enjoyable, then it is nothing. Enjoyment is not necessarily to be equated with laughter. The Greeks had a theory about tragedy which involved the idea of purification through terror. However, it is necessary to state the converse of the previous remark. If theatre concentrates simply and solely on entertainment, then its magic loses its power. Its ritual becomes meaningless and the art of the actor goes into decline.

Finally let us examine another vestigial ritual described by Dr Southern which occurs in the Bavarian Alps on the eve of St Nicholas's Day. The Wild Men appear through the dusk, they wear costumes of animal skins, which distort their figures, and headdresses with horns and antlers. It is difficult to recognize them, although they are all natives of the village. They knock at doors, tap at windows, claim kisses from the girls and, if they catch a girl out of her house, she is chased through the snow by them. It is accepted that the Wild Men remain in control of the village until dawn but, beyond that, there is no script, no performance. What we have here is something that can be fun in itself and is just the shadow of what was once something much more elaborate and complex. It is as if a folk memory had nearly faded away. It is the beginning of theatre, but it never developed at all. But just because it has become formalized we can see that it contains essential theatre as a special occasion on which one person assumes a disguise and, having done so, is willingly accorded special powers by his audience. And the whole thing is rather fun.

With this in mind, let us refer once more to Peter Brook who, in the same book *The Empty Space,* says that if one man, watched by another, crosses an empty space, that is the beginning of theatre. But who is this watcher? In true ritual, all participate to some degree or other, no one watches merely. So far we have not considered the audience, nor made provision for it. This is 'theatre without theatre', in that there are no buildings. The costumed player's acting space remains empty, in his own village, and open to the sky.

3
Early Religious Festivals:
—the West————————

So far we have been concerned with the actor's art emerging, with the other arts, in small communities under primitive conditions.

Obviously we are still only considering beginnings. If we accept that civilization can be said to be nine thousand years old, our next task is to try to find out what contribution the actor has been making to the various civilizations that have flourished during this time. In the next chapters we will consider the growth of the theatre arts in relation to the culture around them.

Western civilization is presumed to have grown out of the Greco-Roman civilization in Europe, which itself grew out of the culture of the Middle East. This culture was not uniform. The three great monotheistic religions of Judaism, Christianity and Islam, tended to exclude the actor. They held that his art was idolatrous and, when it involved the impersonation of the Deity, blasphemous. It is true that the ancient Israelites had dramatic rituals centring around their king, and we must remember that King David was himself a poet and musician who 'danced before the Ark'. With the Exile, in 586 BC, the kingship fell into disrepute and the ritual, and therefore the drama around it, was suppressed. It was, as we shall see, a thousand years before Christianity began seriously to use the actor's skills and very much later before the Jews began to accept drama at all.

EGYPT

The Greco-Roman contribution is large and well documented and we shall consider that presently, but some scholars believe that the origins of Greek theatre lie in Ancient Egypt, so it is in that direction that we shall first look. The difficulties of research inevitably give rise to controversy. Very little is known for certain about Egyptian drama. Some authorities call attention to various hieroglyphic texts which suggest that the Egyptians may have had drama of a sort but there is no archaeological evidence of any theatre building as such.

The Greek historian, Herodotus, has described rituals with some sort of dramatic element in them and there was also a daily temple ritual in which the god was awakened, bathed, anointed, dressed and fed. This could be cited as an example of some sort of drama, but it does also

25

conjure up the rather grotesque picture of dignified grown men solemnly handling life size dolls in a manner more reminiscent of children's play than the beginnings of great theatre!

Nevertheless, according to Professor Fairman, in *The Triumph of Horus* there was at least one example of great drama in Ancient Egypt. To understand the circumstances, we must know a little about the politics of the time. In about 100 BC, the Ptolemies who ruled Egypt happened to be foreign conquerors from the north. This made them vulnerable. They were wise enough not to interfere with the local religion, but this wisdom played into the hands of the crafty priesthood who persuaded them to subsidize political and religious propaganda against their own rule. The form this propaganda took was a dramatic performance. The script of the play—the very first authenticated script in the history of mankind—had been engraved upon the walls of the Temple of Edfu in about 110 BC, but it was then already at least eleven hundred years old. It was called *The Triumph of Horus* and it tells of a ritual battle in which the hero-king harpoons and kills a hippopotamus-demon. It is complete with dialogue and stage directions and illustrations of the characters and it has been translated by Professor Fairman, whose book about it is fascinating to read and includes an account of a 'revival' of the play, at Padgate College of Education in 1971. (This must be a record for the amount of time elapsing between first performance and revival in translation.)

The play seem to have been performed at great annual festivals which lasted for five days. Everyone, without exception, seems to have been free to attend. Food, drink, side shows with singers, dancers and acrobats were provided gratis. A raised space in front of a temple had been cleared and, in front of it, a pit had been dug to represent a certain Sacred Lake. The real lake and its temple were not far away but were unsuitable for the presentation of public spectacle to a large audience and the lake itself would have been too deep for any hippopotamus, real or simulated. From the point of view of the priests, the most important thing was to have as large a crowd as possible. Professor Fairman points out that, strictly speaking, this gathering was not so much an audience as a rough, undisciplined, participating crowd—more like the fans at a football match than our tidy and orderly contemporary theatre audiences.

This disorderly but participating mob was what the priests wanted. The play itself was so written to enable them to keep control. The content is very simple. The villain is Seth, the hippopotamus demon, who happens to be known to the audience as the god of the desert, of foreign lands and of evil. (So he is neatly associated in their minds with the foreign and, therefore, to them, evil king.) In the mythology of Egypt, Seth was brother to Osiris, father to Horus. Seth, just like all the wicked uncles there ever were, slew Osiris and, therefore, had to be killed in his turn by the son of Osiris, that is to say, by Horus who in this way regains his kingdom. The reigning kings could not speak Egyptian and they were, therefore, in a unique position to be misled into thinking that the excitement of the crowd was a demonstration of loyalty to them when it was, in fact, the opposite. Each scene in the early part of the play ends with a chorus, taken up by the onlookers—'Hold fast, Horus, hold fast!', as Horus goes through the various stages of the battle. Once the hippopotamus has been killed, he has to be cut up to be ritually eaten. The play is markedly static and repetitive, as far as the principal characters are concerned, but there is a large chorus who also work as political cheerleaders. The very large audience might not have heard all the words but, knowing the story, they could respond to the patterns of rhythm and the changing tone colour of the speeches.

The Triumph of Horus appears to be the only Ancient Egyptian play actually to be performed but some authorities have called attention to certain hieroglyphics which could be a dramatic text of some kind. This is usually referred to as the Abydos or Osiris Passion Play and is based on a ceremony dating from 2500 BC. Some historians claim that there were strong links between both drama and religions of Egypt and of Greece, via the Middle East; but this is not proven beyond dispute. However, it is from the Middle East that in about 1000 BC a new religion emerged—a religion of great importance to our story.

THE GREEKS

Of all the gods whom the actor has served, it is surely Dionysus who must earn his greatest gratitude, for it was the rituals associated with this Greek god of wine and fertility that gave rise to the first, and perhaps the greatest, drama that has ever been. Great drama has arisen from other religions in other places at other times, as this book testifies but what happened in Greece, especially in the sixth century BC, was both extraordinary and wonderful. Out of semi-barbaric rituals conducted on dark hillsides, and out of the obscene and drunken festivals of their rustic ancestors, the Greeks made the new art form that we now call theatre. The very word is of their making. We cannot discuss acting or plays or theatre building or dramatic criticism without, sooner or later, using words of Greek origin.

Between 550 BC and 300 BC, the art of poetic drama was worked out by the first master playwrights in tragedy and comedy; the acting profession, already established, evolved techniques for the making and use of costume, mask and properties; great theatres were built to contain audiences numbered by the thousand. The wonder is not merely that all this was happening for the first time but that, when it happened, it was so superlatively good. We shall attempt an explanation of the causes of this excellence before we end this chapter but we must first make a very general survey of the periods in the development of Greek theatre. Then we shall concentrate on each in its turn. There seem to be four such periods, overlapping and merging but sufficiently distinct to be characteristic. (The terminology used to name them is derived from various authorities and will be explained as we go along.)

The periods we shall discuss are as follows:

1 Dionysiac, or Ritual, beginning with the arrival of the cult of Dionysus

in Greece in antique times and ending about 550 BC, by which time the professional actor has emerged, theatres have been built, generally of wood and trapezoidal in shape. The period ends with the establishment of the first play-writing contests.

2   Athenian or Classical—the period of the great tragic poets— *Aeschylus (525—456 BC), Sophocles (495—406 BC), Euripides (480—406 BC)* and the comic poet *Aristophanes (448—380 BC).* The contests continue, with comedy included from 486 BC. Theatres such as that of Dionysus at Athens are built and, later, rebuilt in stone. rebuilt in stone.

The Athenian period can be considered as over by 300 BC. Philosophers are paying attention to the arts. *Aristotle (384—322 BC)* writes the *Poetics,* laying down rules for writing plays.

3   The Hellenistic or Colonial period overlaps the Athenian by fifty years or more. Theatres are being built in Greek colonies around the Mediterranean. The shape of the performance area changes. Tragedy is less popular. Comedy changes style from Old (Aristophanic) Comedy (bawdy, critical, politically satirical) to New Comedy (ancestor of modern comedy of manners). The greatest exponent of this is *Menander (343—292 BC).* Although the theatre buildings of this period are often regarded as being typically Greek, they are very different from the buildings in which the Classical Athenian playwrights saw their own works presented. It is very important to realize that changes in materials, structure and ground plan frequently lagged behind innovations within the theatre arts themselves. Also, it must be remembered that Greek civilization extended beyond Athens and endured, although in decline, well into the Christian era. However, there was theatrical activity which took place apart from the great amphitheatres of the period. This was the comic drama known as the Phlyakes (about 43—380 BC), often depicted on vase-paintings and performed on temporary booth stages. (See below and Chapter 5).

4   The Greco-Roman period merges into the previous period at about 250 BC and itself merges into the Roman about the first century AD. The dominant playwrights, *Plautus (250—184 BC)* and *Terence (190—159 BC)* wrote in Latin but, almost certainly, from Greek models. By 55 BC Pompey's Playhouse in Rome, with its strictly semicircular auditorium, is set up as the true Roman theatre and the glory of Greece has gone into the dust.

At this point we must issue a warning. Neither Greeks nor Romans were conservationists. They tended to knock theatres down and rebuild them without thought for historians to come. So archaeological evidence for the entire Greek period is both scarce and misleading. Other evidence is also scanty. Most of the plays and much of the philosophical and other writings of the Greeks were lost. Many modern authorities base their descriptions of Greek theatres upon the writings of *Vitruvius,* but we must remember that he did not 'publish' until about the year 150 BC. He is credited with the statement that Aeschylus was the inventor of painted scenery but such a remark needs to be treated with caution.

Pollux, another Latin writer two hundred years later than Vitruvius, is the source of much information about masks. It should be remembered that he may be describing things that pertain to the later periods rather than to classic Athenian times.

We will now take each period in turn for closer examination.

Dionysiac ritual

In the very beginning there were neither theatres nor plays, merely open spaces on which people met at certain times of the year, in accordance with the seasonal requirements of the culture of the grape, to worship Dionysus.

Dionysus was a foreign god, made acceptable to the Greeks by adaptation of myth to make him a son of Zeus. He has many names and attributes. Some call him Bacchus and his Greek name means 'twice born'. Statues sometimes depict him as a portly old man and sometimes as a beautiful youth. As god of wine he made men feel cheerful in the face of hardship, but he could also inflame them to madness and self destruction. As nature god he was attended by strange creatures, the satyrs, who were half human, half animal. As god of fertility he presided over rites involving an oversize representation of the human phallus. In all that it is easy to see no more than yet another nature ritual of the type described in the previous chapters. (Indeed, some modern writers suggest that Greek drama is derived directly from seasonal rituals without any reference to Dionysus.)

Be that as it may, the origins of both the satyr play, which burlesqued the tragedies, and the bawdy backchat of the Old Comedy are quite apparent. But how did all this rustic clumping about lead to the grandeur of Greek tragedy? In the first place, we must never forget that Dionysus, for all his association with wine and merriment, was not to be treated lightly. He could, as we have already mentioned, send people mad and lead them to do horrible things in their madness. All nature religions have their sinister aspects and these certainly appear in the content of Greek tragedy. The main link, however, between a religion and the drama arising from it must be in the *form* of the ceremonies themselves. For instance, the absence of dance from a dominant position in medieval religious drama in Europe arises simply out of the absence of dance as part of the church services of the time. Likewise, the dominance of dance in much Asiatic drama arises from the fact that the first Asiatic religious ceremonies took the form of dance. (See Chapter 4) Thus it was with the Greeks, the centre of whose ceremonies was the *dithyramb*, a choric hymn sung by a chorus and incorporating mimes and dances depicting incidences in the life of the god himself and culminating in the sacrifice of a goat. The word tragedy is derived from the Greek words meaning goat-song.

As years passed, the interest of the participants shifted from *what* was being done to *how* it was being done. Specialists emerged as they always will when some activity has been well established. The clumsy left the dancing to the more agile; the tone deaf gave up singing to concentrate on the possibilities of the mime. Many decided to opt out from all activity to watch and, perhaps, to criticize. A fundamental dichotomy was about to occur, but we cannot yet speak of a division between actors and audience. Rather, the whole group remained one congregation still. They were all engaged in the act of worship, with some being active and others passive, content to let others intercede with the god on their behalf.

Nearest to the god, stood the leader of the chorus. Originally, perhaps, the leader had been a civic dignitary, the head man, but when it became apparent that political wisdom was no guarantee of talent, then the *coryphaeus*, as he was called, was expected to be a performer of outstanding talent.

For countless years, every *coryphaeus* seems to have remained content to be chorus-leader and narrator of the story of the god, but on some glorious but unrecorded occasion one of them must have taken the step from *narration* to *impersonation*. The ritual became truly dramatic. Instead of merely referring to the god in the third person, past tense ('Then Dionysus did this...') he spoke as Dionysus in the first person, present tense ('Behold, I am Dionysus! Watch what I do now!')

Tradition says that the first person to do this was a certain Thespis of Ikaria in Attica, a poet who wrote for, and perhaps led a group of, professional actors who travelled around on a cart, which they also used as a platform. (If this tradition is true, then perhaps there was already secular drama of some sort. We sometimes have the feeling that the costumed player and his travelling stage may indeed be older than time itself!) Having introduced the first actor, Thespis must also have brought the first mask into use in the service of Dionysus. We shall discuss the mask in detail later but it was obviously necessary for the actor's impersonation.

The competitive festivals

Whether Thespis is half-traditional or not, it is believed that he was the first winner of the public contest for tragic poets in 534 BC in Athens.

The setting-up of these competitive festivals, sponsored by the government, encouraged the flowering of the theatre arts which was so marked in the classical Athenian age. Poets were encouraged to write and submit their tragedies and, later (in 486 BC), their comedies. Actors and choruses were recruited and paid to participate. The poets usually acted as 'directors' but the function of the impresario, involving the payment of all expenses except the salaries of the cast, was undertaken by wealthy citizens chosen by lot. Most of these regarded the task as an honour and in any case the *choregus*, as the impresario was called, was the official recipient of any prize. These contests were great events, beginning at dawn on the appropriate day of the festival. When we recall that each poet submitted four plays (three tragedies and a satyr play) we realize that the entertainment must have lasted for a very long time. They were watched by crowds even bigger than the largest First Division football crowds of today. Drama had outgrown its birthplace on the communal threshing floor.

The changing shape of the theatre

The dancing place, the area around the altar of Dionysus, was known as the *orchestra*, and it was usually at the foot of the slope. (Mountainous Greece had theatres on natural slopes. The Romans, as we shall see, had to use their skill in building arches.)

There is no universal agreement among the authorities as to the exact process by which the simple dancing place evolved into the Greek theatre. Some, like Nicoll (see Bibliography) presume that the orchestra was circular from the very beginning. Then, it is said, there followed a period of temporary provision ending with the building of stone theatres with the 'typical' fan-shaped (more than semi-circular) auditorium as early as the beginning of the fifth century BC at Athens. Other writers, notably Leacroft (see Bibliography), suggest a process by which the stone fan-shape does not appear until the fourth century BC, in the second theatre of Dionysus at Athens.

These writers presume that there were performances in towns as well as in the countryside and that these performances would have taken place in the *agora* or market place and not on a threshing floor. These market places would tend to be rectangular, therefore the early town orchestras would be rectangular also, with terraced seating along one side. It certainly seems reasonable to suppose that, as increasing populations made for increasing audiences, then the terraces would have to extend back to their limits and also, later, curve horsehoe-wise around the acting area. All writers agree that, by the Hellenistic period, theatres had taken the 'typical shape', so often illustrated, as in the third theatre of Dionysus (330 BC), ruins of which still remain.

As the theatre buildings grew to accommodate audiences, they also changed to meet the needs of both poets and players. The resources of the player, we remember, include his costume, his mask, his stage and his 'place'. At Athens, each of these resources, in its own development, had its effect on the others. We have seen how the mask became necessary as soon as the actor began to impersonate a god or a hero, but the increasing size of the audiences made it impossible to convey changes of mood effectively, so one character would need several masks. On the other hand, it became possible for one actor to play several characters. Changes of mask implied the need of a place in which the actor could change and where he could keep masks and costumes that were not in use—in short, for a dressing room, as near as possible to the action but where actors could be hidden from the audience.

Simultaneously there were two other needs—a background to play against, and some means of representing the whereabouts of the action. All these needs were met by the erection of a simple tent (later a hut) behind the orchestra. The side facing the audience could be painted to represent a location, and the actor could change inside. This tent was called the *skena*, which, in conjunction with orchestra and auditorium through many variations, remains a principal component of any theatre built in the three thousand years since the Greeks.

As yet there was no stage in the modern sense of the word but, as the function of the actors became more obviously separate from that of the chorus, architectural provision came to be made. Allowing for differences in time-scale between the authorities mentioned above, it is safe to say that perhaps in the Athenian and certainly in the Hellenistic period the *skena* were no longer temporary huts but solid stone and major architectural features of all Greek theatres. It was not long before the playwrights saw their possibilities and began to set the location of their plays not, as previously, in open spaces or deserts but outside temples or palaces or at the gates of a great city. By about 425 BC the *skena* became extended on the side facing the audience into a continuous wall ending in projecting wings, called *paraskenia*. Between these wings there was a long stage set above orchestra level, and it was called the *logeion* or 'speaking place' to distinguish it from the orchestra or dancing place. The actor was beginning to separate himself even more from the chorus and this separation was encouraged by the later playwright-poets of the Athenian period and even more so by the writers of the New Comedy in the early Hellenistic period.

As if to underline the distinction, the actors entered in character, dressed and masked, through one of the three doors (the *thyromata*) from the *skena* on to the *logeion*, while the chorus continued to enter from round the side of the *skena* on ground floor level through passage ways known as *parados*. The *logeion*, which may have been originally quite low, may have risen, in Hellenistic and later times, until it was some ten or twelve feet above orchestra level and supported on pillars. What was originally no more than a blank frontage of a simple tent or hut (the

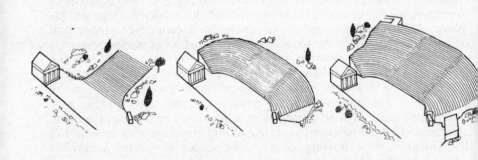

One theory for the development of the Greek amphitheatre — starting from the simple 'end stage' with the audience on one side and then, with increasing numbers of spectators, the gradual envelopment of the acting area

skena) had become elaborated into this pillared structure called the *proskenion*. The word simply means 'front of the *skena*,' but we recommend care in the use of this term, partly because authorities differ as to its exact definition and partly because, while it is the ancestor of the modern word proscenium, the two structures are architecturally different. Suffice it to say that by about 300 BC the actors had been raised up on to a sort of stage.

The *proskenion*, by Greco-Roman times and perhaps earlier, may have begun to to present a two-storey appearance. There may have been a place above, the *theologeion* on which the gods appeared and spoke. In any case the actors are now well raised up and always visible above the chorus. On the roof of the *skena* structure there may have been a crane which would be used to lower a god to the ground level when, as *deus ex machina*, he interfered directly with human affairs.

There is controversy as to how far the Greeks used painted scenery. In spite of Vitruvius, our own guess is that Aeschylus used very little. Euripides and Aristophanes may have used machinery. There is internal evidence in the plays to suggest that the comic poet parodied the tragedian by using one of his situations which depends upon a crane which goes wrong. Increasingly through the Hellenistic and Greco-Roman periods 'special effects' are likely to have been used in increasingly spectacular performances. Loss of discipline in writing led to excesses in production. Whereas in the classic Athenian period horrid murders, etc, took place off stage and were solemnly narrated by the actor who played the part of Second Messenger; in later times a tableau would be set up in a rather grisly 'wax museum' style on a platform and wheeled into the orchestra. The platform was called the *ekkyklema*. Some authorities say that painted panels, to show scenery, were mounted between the pillars of the *proskenion* and also that triangular prisms, the *periaktoi*, were set at the side of the action and revolved to indicate changes of location.

The actors

During these hundreds of years of change, what was happening to the actor? As we have seen he begins by doing very well, receiving a state salary for performing at the Dionysia, but also having the opportunity to take private engagements as well. These Dionysia were festivals held seasonally in honour of the god Dionysus. They varied in character according to time of the year and differed between city and country, but they were always great occasions lasting for days and frequently including performances of all kinds. In Hellenistic times he doubtless appeared in the broad secular comedies played in the booth stages. (See above and Phylax Chapter 6 pages 66-67.)

The classical Athenian period is one of the high peaks in the historical progression of the costumed player and, after the initial explosion of energy, there is a long slow decline from the fourth century onwards. In his great early days his prime personal resource was undoubtedly his appearance. In his high boots (the *kothurnus*) and his headdress (the *onkos*), a six foot actor would appear to be seven feet six inches in height. His very simple flowing garment (the *chiton*) was padded, to prevent him from appearing too thin. The impression already created is of a gigantic figure moving slowly and with dignity against the pale sky of very early morning. The *onkos* and *chiton* had symbolic qualities. Variations in the height of the headdress indicated differences in rank. Patterns and colours on the *chiton* indicated character and mood of the wearer. So it was easy for an audience to recognize characters as soon as they appeared.

The mask

We have already mentioned the mask. It would be an exaggeration to claim that these had any great megaphonic power. In any case the theatres of the time appeared to have an excellent acoustic, because of their bowl shape and, more particularly, the very dry atmosphere of Attic Greece. However, it is the mask that completes our picture of the typical Greek actor, the basic masks of comedy and tragedy with their wide mouths—upturned for comedy and downturned for tragedy—that have become symbols for the art of theatre throughout the world. As we have seen, its first use was to permit one actor to play many parts and the three actors that came to make a Greek company were able to play many more—including, we must not forget, all female parts as well as male.

More than that, the mask maintained the continuity with the ritual and religious roots of the actor's art. After all, it is presumptuous of any mortal man to impersonate a god or even a hero. He must first become anonymous behind his mask. It also provided each actor with a repertoire of instantly recognizable characterization. The writer, Pollux, (see above) records over thirty different types of masks used in tragedy and many more in comedy. There are many illustrations of these and it is interesting to compare the faces with the conventional types developed later in the theatre. This leads to interesting speculations about human nature and also about the actor's basic skill in first observing and then imitating.

The chorus

We cannot leave the Greeks without some mention of the role and function of the *chorus* as costumed players. Tragedy owes much of its grandeur to their presence, whether in stately procession, ritual dance, or those terrifying moments when they stand stock-still. Old Comedy gained in colour from the disguises of the two choruses. Aristophanes called for wasps, birds, frogs and many other strange creatures. He also got comic effect from having the two choruses hurl insults and other things at each other in the *Lysistrata*, when the old men face the old women.

The chorus had a long and honourable history. Arion and Lesbos set the number for the tragic chorus at fifty by the beginning of the sixth century BC, but Aeschylus reduced it drastically to twelve. Sophocles increased it to fifteen at which it stayed until its decline. As we have seen, during the

Hellenistic and Greco-Roman periods, it became less and less important in both comedy and tragedy. It was perhaps the most obvious link with the ritual origins of Greek drama so it is to be expected that, as drama became more secular, the orchestra (originally the dance place) would become less important than the *logeion* (the speaking place) and thus it was.

THE ROMANS

If we look beyond the theatres to the general political history of the time, we note that during the latter part of the period we have been discussing, the Greeks were spreading their civilization through the Mediterranean, by a process of colonization. With the decline of the Greek city states, and the rise of the Roman Empire, a different process takes place.

The new Roman colonists carried their way of life beyond the Mediterranean, as far afield as Britain, and one of the institutions they took with them was the theatre, which they had been given by the Greeks. There was no sudden break; no date at which we can say Greek theatre ceased and Roman theatre began but by 55 BC Pompey's playhouse, in Rome itself, had established a new model. During the period of overlap, between the two cultures, we note inevitable similarities between the theatres of Greece and Rome but, increasingly, marked differences.

If one of the master playwrights of Athens could have been transported into a Roman playhouse in the first century BC he might, at first, have been impressed by the architectural coherence and efficiency of the playhouse itself, but other things might have puzzled him. While there might have been a shrine to one of the Roman gods inside the theatre itself, as the Greeks had had the altar of Dionysus, there would not have been any priest present, nor any obeissance to the gods, nor indeed any mention of them at all. Secularization of the theatre had become complete under Roman rule. Even though the performance might have taken place on a day dedicated to one or other of the gods, the religious occasion was simply an excuse to have a holiday and to enjoy an entertainment. An example from our own secularized theatre would be the performance of a pantomine at Christmas—an entertainment which cannot be said in any way to celebrate the nativity.

The buildings

The next difference our Athenian would note would be in the theatre building itself. The Romans had begun, as did the Greeks, with wooden structures but these had been very soon replaced by permanent stone buildings, usually financed by public money. The auditorium generally remained semi-circular but was not built on sloping ground. The Roman genius for arches made it possible for them to construct a series of terraces for seating. The orchestra, now an acting rather than a dancing area, had been reduced in size, reflecting the diminution and eventual disappearance of the chorus. Indeed, it had become a custom for wealthy members of the audience to buy privileged seats within the acting area itself. The stage was both wider and deeper, thus encroaching still more upon the orchestra. The Romans latinized the Greek *proskenion* into *proscaenium* and seem to have used the word to mean the whole of the acting area and its background. This background was called the *scaenae frons* and was elaborately colonnaded, with statues on plinths. It was two or three storeys in height and was pierced by two or three practical doors. We shall meet this style again later, when it was copied by the Renaissance architect-designers. The terminology is a little confusing but it is necessary to remember that the *proskenion* is not the same as the *proscaenium* and that neither is the same as the *scaenae frons*.

The *parados*, the passage used in common by both audience and chorus as an entrance, had been abolished and the audience now entered from the back, at the highest level. Behind the *proscaenium*, there are not only dressing rooms but large spaces devoted to the storage of costumes, props and stage machinery. In other words, the Roman theatre of this period was very like some post-Renaissance theatres of Western Europe up to, and including, the early twentieth century. (There are, however, very important exceptions to this statement which will be discussed in Chapter 8).

The Athenian visitor might well have been pleased with the theatre. As a playwright he would have been aware of the possibilities for special effects. Part of the acting area, for instance, could be walled off and flooded for aquatic displays. Other technical effects, mainly inherited from the Greeks, would also have been at his disposal. As to scenery, there is more documentary than archaeological evidence. Some writers seem to imply that there was painted scenery, but this is not certain. There are similar controversies over the question as to whether or not Roman theatres had a curtain in front of the stage. Some authorities state categorically that there was such a device which was hauled up from a slot in the ground to cover the scene and lowered to reveal it. It was a wooden shutter rather than a curtain and was there, it is said, not so much to mask the scene as to protect the audience from wild animals that took part in the performances. If so, then this is probably the first example in the history of theatre of a safety curtain! (The Roman theatre at St Albans had such a curtain slot.)

The plays

Our early Greek may well have been disappointed in the play itself. Both tragedy and comedy, as he knew them, were gone. It is very unlikely that tragedies in the Athenian style were ever performed in the Roman theatre. (Seneca would be writing about a hundred years later, but his verse tragedies were intended to be read, and perhaps declaimed, but not to be acted). The comedies bore some resemblance to Greek New Comedy but lacked the elements of parody and political satire. These comedies are concocted to appeal to as wide an audience as possible by including such features as complications of plot, stock comic business, exploitation of extremely marked characteristics, topical jokes and indecency. A modern analogy would be the *Carry on* series of films. The American musical *A Funny Thing Happened on the way to the Forum* was based on Roman original scripts. It is only fair to note that the players themselves were probably as talented as their modern equivalents. Something had happened to public taste in Rome.

Whether or not the Roman writers wished to write in this style, we shall never know, except that we have the evidence of a later writer of comedies, Publius Terence, that he was in constant fear of losing his audiences to other entertainments being offered. Because it was the custom of the Roman authorities to site all their public amenities close to each other, so that the forum, public baths, etc, were adjacent to the theatre, the circus or amphitheatre might be literally next door. This meant, as Terence says, that his own audience could be lured away very quickly to watch some new acrobats or dare-devil riders. In consequence the theatre tried to rival the circus with its own spectacular shows and animal acts. We must remember that it was the Romans who were responsible for the piece of political wisdom that suggests that a disaffected public can be kept happy with 'bread and circuses'.

To return to our early Athenian in the Roman theatre, perhaps his greatest shock would come after the performance when he went behind to talk to the actors. He would already have noted certain similarities with his own theatre, such as the use of masks and of colour symbolism, but the differences would have appalled him, most of all when he discovered that the player was not a free citizen but a slave, despised by the community, not respected as he would have been in Greek theatre. The players' master would have been an impresario, a business-man producer who would have no motive other than making a profit by selling seats in a theatre, in competition with other spectacular entertainments.

As the Roman Empire fell into decay (assisted by such show-business?) and Europe entered the period known as The Dark Ages, we must consider what effect this had upon the theatre arts. Seneca, a major poet, was writing but was not performed. The players, even if called upon to perform his work, would not be likely to understand it or know how to act it. A major division had occurred between two sides of theatre art. The playwright and the actor became estranged and remained so for hundreds of years; for the public, entertainment is everything. Something had been lost from the theatre.

4
Early Religious Festivals:
—the East

Until comparatively recently there was a tendency, here in the West, to regard the theatres of the Orient as being no more than a special case of primitive theatre that had acquired technique and elaboration merely through having been in existence for a long time. There were several barriers to our comprehension, arising from differences in religion and very marked differences in the conventions of performance.

It is salutary to remember, though, that in spite of all their great achievements, the theatre artists of the West are massively outnumbered by those of the East. Not only are there more people in Asia than in Europe but, throughout Asia, almost every village has a regular theatrical performance as part of its normal religious life. If we combine Brahminism/Hinduism with Buddhism, and include the almost infinite number of local religions which are linked with one or other of these, then the adherents of these religions far outnumber the Christians of the world.

The age of the two cultures is comparable. Buddhism is now two thousand five hundred years old and Brahminism a thousand years older. The basic collections of myths and legends which have become part of the literature of the East, such as the *Ramayana* and the *Mahabharata*, compare with the *Odyssey*, the *Iliad* and the *Old Testament*. Furthermore, not only is the practice of religion inextricably inter-connected with the practice of the theatre arts but, according to myth, the creation of the world was itself an act of theatre. The Lord Shiva danced and in dancing created the world. To this day one of his titles is 'Lord of the Dance' and he is the Indian god of Creation and Destruction.

INDIA

In the crowded cities and across the wide rural plains of India, China, Japan and South East Asia there have arisen many different kinds of performance. There are also marked similarities, not only among the Eastern actors themselves but between them and the costumed players of the West.

Theatre in India seems to have followed a similiar pattern to the Greek in that as long ago as 1500 BC, in the period of the Vedic hymns, ceremonies were held in which narrative verse, in praise of gods, was

38

declaimed. The move from narration about gods and heroes to their impersonation in drama occurs in the epic period 500 BC to 320 BC. The plays were written in Sanskrit and include the *Ramayana* which is still being performed to this very day throughout the whole of India and elsewhere in the Orient. Every October a great festival is held, the main event of which is the performance of this cycle of plays.

The story has in it the classic elements of married love tested by separation, usurpation of kingship, journeys and adventures and protracted battles with demons. There are two kinds of principal characters, four of whom are sacred—Rama, his wife and two brothers—and the others are secular although supernatural—Ravanna, the King of the demons, and Hanuman, the Monkey King, who is Rama's ally against the demons. He has his own troubles but also provides much of the comedy in the story.

We are indebted to the BBC for the following documentation of different kinds of performance of this play, taking place during October 1979, in different parts of India.

The first of these probably approximates most closely to the traditional style of performance. It was at Benares, sponsored by the Maharajah. It was set not in a theatre but in a wide open space and played in nightly instalments. Each performance lasted for about half-an-hour and was a major part of the evening's festivities. The four sacred characters were played by boys, specially chosen for the parts. For the duration of the feast, they were accorded the same respect that would have been given to their prototypes. It is said that, in the past, to be so selected was deemed to be such an honour that nothing in this life could possibly equal it. So, at the end of the final performance, the boy actors were given drinks containing poison. This may sound cruel but we must remember that, by Brahmin reasoning, it would give them the chance to be reborn immediately into more fortunate circumstances. It is worth noting that the one female part, of Rama's wife Sita, is also played by one of the boys.

Their costume is simple and usually white. Their make-up is traditional, taking a long time to put on and needing sequins as well as paint. The Maharajah himself attends every performance, on the back of an elephant in traditional style. At the conclusion of the whole cycle of plays, members of his royal house greet and do obeissance to the four boy actors.

If we remember that Benares is a holy city, then these performances would parallel a revival of a Greek tragic cycle in the theatre of Dionysus in Athens in the presence of the Head of State. In contrast, the same cycle of plays performed in a village has some similarities in its organization to the English mystery cycle as played by the guilds. For instance, it is traditional for the same part to be played by one actor for many successive years so that the actor playing, for example, the Monkey King, would be as well known by the name of his role as he would be by his own name. Audiences are smaller and the style of playing perhaps more rough than in the Maharajah's production but it is no less enjoyable to all concerned.

In South India, the same story receives very different treatment again from the professional Kathakali dancers. These have served an arduous apprenticeship from the age of seven, a great deal of it spent in rigorous exercise of facial muscles and in hand movements. Since the dialogue is spoken, or rather intoned, in Sanskrit, a language now not understood by the great majority of the people, a unique grammar of dance has been invented. By this means the actor can by movement act complete sequence of sentences in time with the spoken narrative. Once the audience have acquired the conventions, they can then 'read' the dancers' movements and so follow the story. That, at least, is the theory. In practice, it is likely that most of the audience are already as familiar with the story as we in the West are with the great Bible stories.

The next example from India is another very marked contrast. This performance of the *Ramayana* was the only one shown taking place inside a building, a western-style theatre, and used many of the appurtenances of the West, such as spotlights and glamourizing make-up. This type of performance, with its crude mixture of debased styles and, although it purports to be a religious celebration, its commercialism, may well remind us of the Roman influence coming in to destroy the Greek tradition.

INDONESIA

Indonesia has made many contributions to theatre arts, the most famous of which is the ritual Barong play, which is described in Chapter 2. This is notable not only for its beauty but as an example of drama arising from the conflict of religions. Some people would say that the benign Barong represents Buddhism and Rangda the older religion of demon-worship. Also the Barong appears to be rather Chinese in appearance whereas Rangda could be a personification of Durga, an Indian Goddess. Racial cultures and religions were in a state of constant ebb and flow throughout Asia and this has naturally affected the theatre.

Another example comes from Java where, after the Moslem conversion of the fifteenth and sixteenth centuries, the actor could no longer practise his craft for fear of committing a blasphemy by impersonation of a sacred person; this led to the celebrated Javanese shadow puppets coming into being, which was permitted by the Moslem rulers. The puppet plays, the *Wajang-kulit*, give us a rather special example of the costumed player at work. Indeed, we shall call the Javanese puppet master a non-costumed player in that he operates stripped to the waist and is, by convention, invisible. Not only does he operate the puppets but he narrates, speaks dialogue and sings for them, in character and with great skill. He literally has his hands full while working but cues the orchestra (the *gamelan*, which is mainly tuned percussion) and has two assistants to feed him the puppets.

Frequently his head is shaved. Since we have said that he is stripped to the waist, he very much resembles a priest. Indeed, he has a symbolic role in the whole drama. The screen on which the shadows appear is equated to Heaven, the stage represents Earth, and the puppet master himself represents God, using the puppets to tell a sacred story. The play itself is usually one of the stories in the Indian *Ramayana* cycle. Once again, we notice a mixture of religious influences.

When the Moslem influence became less, two other theatres grew up and have continued parallel with the *Wajang-kulit*. One of these is a three dimensional doll-puppet theatre, which might have come from China or Japan, and the other the *Wajang-orang*, that is to say the people play. Live actors were permitted once more to perform in public, but both the stories and the way they were enacted were very much in imitation of the original puppet play.

Of course Indonesia, like the rest of Asia, has been subjected to strong Western influences and, on one of the islands, this has gone so far as to bring about the adoption of Western stories into the Eastern repertoire. One of the great favourites, we understand, is a *Wajang-orang* play called *Hamlet!*

JAPAN

The classical theatre of Japan, the Noh Theatre, like most Asiatic theatre, had its origin in religious ritual. As with the Indian theatre, there is a rather charming legend about it. It is said theatre had its beginnings when the Shinto sun goddess felt sad and shut herself away from the world in a cave. The world became dark and cold, so the other gods went to the mouth of the cave to try to persuade her to come out. They decided to gladdden her heart by performing a ritual dance. One of the goddesses broke a branch from the cherry tree and danced and sang, moving the branch with graceful gestures. In this way, the legend says, the Noh theatre was born.

The Noh has many features both in form and content which closely resemble those of Greek and Buddhist theatre; the actors are always male and many are masked; the elements of dance and song are as important as narration and dialogue and the stories are largely concerned with supernatural powers. The Noh theatre appears to have developed around the end of the fourteenth century, although the earliest known texts date from 1600. Some 250 play texts are extant and are still performed today in very much the same way as they were some 400 years ago and it is this fact which makes them, and the methods of presentation associated with them, of particular interest to the theatre historian—it is almost as if the plays of the Elizabethan dramatists were still being played in the original productions on a form of the original stage! The traditional Noh stage, still in use today, consists of a platform some 20 feet square and 3 feet high, surmounted by a roof supported on four pillars. This is the main acting space and the audience sits on two sides of this platform, the other two sides having extensions or 'verandahs' which are occupied by the musicians and the stage attendants. From one corner of this free standing acting area a long bridge some three feet wide complete with railings connects the stage with the 'offstage' areas and along this both actors and

Japanese Kabuki theatre showing actor on the flower walk (hanamichi)

musicians make their entrances. No scenery is used and the plays are a mixture of dancing, chanting and recitative with relatively little dialogue and are performed by two principal actors, one of whom is usually masked. Noh performances have always appealed primarily to an educated upper-class audience and it was inevitable that a more popular form of theatre would evolve; this in fact did occur and is known as Kabuki and, like Noh, is still performed today in very much its traditional form. Although taking much of its material and style from the Noh, the Kabuki theatre is very different in its presentation methods. The stage is wide and shallow with the audience seated in front of it—in the twentieth century buildings there is even a proscenium opening in western style—and from the front left hand corner (as seen from the audience) a long bridge some three feet wide runs out to the back of the auditorium. This is the famous *hana-michi* or 'flower walk' along which actors make entrances and exits and even perform some parts of the action. Unlike the Noh theatre, Kabuki makes great use of spectacular scenery, including the use of a revolve to change sets, but the actors are not masked and some of the action is relatively naturalistic and the language modern. Music and dance play an equally important part in Kabuki theatre but many more than two actors are used with spectacular costumes and effects which make it a very popular form of entertainment.

CHINA

The theatre of China is traditionally dated from 2500 BC arising out of religious ceremonies mainly in the form of dance. According to Chinese historians, during the Shang dynasty 1766 to 1122 BC, these dances were a part of ceremonies in honour of the gods controlling rain and drought and also harvest and famine. They were not public performances. The audiences were limited to the Emperor, his court and the appropriate priests—and, presumably, the gods themselves. The whole proceedings were not thought of as entertainment but as ritual, as a symbolic offering to the gods in the hope of rain and harvest rather than drought and famine. (In other parts of the world food, wine libations, human sacrifices even, were offered for similar purposes).

Since those days, the theatre arts of China have grown and proliferated into a great variety of forms but, in spite of all influences, the main stream has remained traditional. The early dance dramas became sacred plays, as with the Greeks, with narration, speech and song as well as dance. The title of 'Father of the Chinese theatre' must go to the Emperor Ming Huang, AD 713-756. It is in his memory that, even today, actors are referred to as 'the children of the pear garden', for it was in such an orchard in his palace grounds that he founded the first professional training theatre in China.

From those days right down to the present there has been a continuous tradition in the recruitment and training of actors. Frequently they were taken into the company as mere babies. Usually these were orphans, babies left abandoned or, in evil times, sold by their parents. Knowing no family but that of the theatre, they learned to move and speak and sing as performers at the same time as they learned to walk and talk.

In classical China, actors were forbidden to enter for the civil service examinations, which were the usual means of promotion. In many ways they were regarded as belonging to the lowest level of society, being quite simply slaves, although slaves to a noble and precious art. They appear to have accepted this valuation by society and to have dedicated themselves to the disciplines of the arts of theatre with the religious fervour of a medieval monk or nun. (Women played on the Chinese stage until the eighteenth century; from then on, in most theatres, the art became exclusively male).

In spite of the westernization and secularization which has occurred in China, in the same way as we have seen it occurring in India, traditional classical theatre persists and flourishes. Even in Communist China the authorities have generally encouraged it for many reasons although, for a time in the early 1970s, during the Cultural Revolution all classical theatre was proscribed, in a manner reminiscent of the excesses of our own English Puritans in the seventeenth century. However, after the death of Mao, in 1976, the tendency was reversed.

In all the religious festivals that we have looked at so far, there are enough similarities to suggest that there may well be a universal pattern in such things. The general buzz of excitement and the atmosphere of holiday merrymaking surrounding the Chinese temple festivals has been described as being very similar to that of an English country fair. There is feasting, followed by a procession up to the temple door led by a dancing lion, much more in the atmosphere of carnival than of solemn rite. The central dramatic performance is surrounded by side shows. This has obvious parallels, not only throughout present-day Asia but in medieval England and in the more comic and drunken aspects of the worship of Dionysus in Ancient Greece.

The temporary booth theatre, made of bamboo and matting and called a Mat shed, is set up to face the temple door. (We shall be making constant reference to the booth stage later in this book, see Chapter 6. The Chinese were probably the first to invent this, as they were the first in other important inventions.) This placing of the stage near the temple reminds us how the Greeks did likewise and how English religious drama actually began inside the walls of the church itself.

It has been said that, in techniques, Chinese traditional theatre stands midway between the Commedia dell' Arte and the Elizabethan professional theatre in England. (We shall later refer, in great detail, to these two great and contrasting styles of acting. For the present it is sufficient if the reader realizes that the basic difference between them is that the Commedia was an actors' theatre, based on improvisation, and that the Elizabethan was a playwright's theatre, based upon story and spoken language.)

The Chinese theatre derives its highly disciplined skills from long and arduous apprenticeship, in a manner similar to that of the Commedia. Both Italian and Chinese actors could claim to be universal specialists in all aspects of their art. They were actors, mimes, acrobats, musicians, singers and dancers *par excellence*. The Chinese went further: they did not specialize in one single role but each actor was—and is today—clown as well as tragedian; character actor or female impersonator as circumstances require.

Unlike the Italian, but more like the English, Chinese plays frequently have great literary merit and beautifully poetic language. In this respect, particularly in the underlying religious and mythological content, they resemble the Athenian plays of the time of Aeschylus.

However, what is essentially Chinese is what can only be called the totality of the theatrical experience they provide, which is based upon a totality of symbolism. To explain this statement we must look back to what is known of the very earliest recorded Chinese theatre. This was an offering to the gods. But which gods? Looking back, we see that they were the gods of rain and harvest and the deities (probably demons) of drought and famine. These may have been merely examples, but we do not think it coincidental that these deities seem to be paired through their opposite properties. Rain and harvest are obviously auspicious and connected; drought and famine inauspicious and connected.

Over the centuries, Asiatic religious and mystic thinking has worked upon the concept of equal and opposite forces throughout the universe. These are usually referred to as Yang, auspicious and positive, and Yin, inauspicious and negative. Many Westerners have become aware of this concept and the religious ideas that stem from it. We do not discuss it in any detail here but, since it has a profound effect on Chinese theatre, we must briefly consider the complexity of the symbolism. For instance there is colour symbolism, red is Yang and white is Yin. So good characters use predominantly red make-up and bad characters predominantly white. Every other colour has its appropriate associations so that a character's age, sex, rank, disposition and character can all be read from his make-up. Similar rules apply to costume and properties.

At first sight this may appear arbitrary and, in any case, it might be thought that such complexity would make it difficult for a stranger to understand what is going on. However, European eye witnesses assure us that this is not so. While the native audience are, naturally, more aware of the subtleties of the performance, the technical skill of the actors makes it certain that any audience will be able to follow the main line. Such a complete symbolism (which extends to the actual aligning of the stage in relation to points of the compass, to animal symbolism, number symbolism and so on) might make for trivial or boring theatre were it not for the totality of the aesthetic effect. The impact is direct. The spectators' senses become under simultaneous attack. Costume, gesture, pose, characterisation, scenery, make-up—all blend with the music and other sound effects to produce what can only be described as total theatre.

First Interlude

FOR THINKING ABOUT RITUAL AND RELIGION IN TERMS OF THEATRE ARTS

Before going on to the possibly more familiar topic of the medieval Christian theatre, we are pausing to look back over the last two chapters to try to clarify any conclusions that may have arisen over the concepts of ritual and religious theatre.

The word ritual is one that we share with scholars in other disciplines such as sociology, anthropology and psychology. All would admit that ritual is a useful but controversial word, so we are going to try to clarify its meaning for ourselves in a way that will give little or no offence to other disciplines. First of all, let us be clear that a ritual act is one in which *symbolic content* of the act is much more important than the act itself. For instance, in the Christian Holy Communion, the priest puts a wafer into the communicant's mouth. The priest is not feeding the communicant in the obvious sense. The action is symbolic and therefore ritual. An act may be a ritual or part of a ritual but it need not be sacred, that is to say it can be totally unconnected with religion. The Trooping of the Colour, the ceremonial use of the Mace in the House of Commons, or even the chanting of certain songs at football matches, can all be held to be ritual behaviour.

We now come to the connection between ritual and art. It used to be presumed that all art arose out of ritual. From this it followed that the symbolic content was originally more important than what we would now call the aesthetic content. Therefore when art came to be practised for its own sake, it lost touch with ritual and with religion. While the previous statement seems reasonable, some experts feel that it may be an over-simplification, particularly when we consider how far some arts today have moved from their original ritual and religious roots. Within the scope of our present study it does seem true, however, that much greater theatre has arisen out of ritual. It would also seem that once the theatre separates itself from religion then there *may* be a decline in the artistic quality of that theatre. It has yet to be proved that there is any direct connection between the aesthetic and the symbolic strengths in the same work of art.

Two other points need to be made. The first is the reasonably simple statement that many great theatres of the world seem to have passed through similar phases of development in organization and the actual physical structure of their performance area and the equipment of their players. Our examples so far suggest that the first two phases coincide with periods in which art is connected to ritual and religion. It does not necessarily follow that this will always be so.

The second point is made to link the previous chapter with the chapter to come, which is concerned with the European religious plays of medieval times. The actors who took part in them share a common view of the universe which was expressed through a common symbolism. Likewise, in the Elizabethan age, actors and audience shared a common symbolism that was as highly detailed in its way as that of the Chinese. It is impossible to understand fully Shakespeare's texts without reference to that symbolism. Although the theatre was divorced from the church it remained dependent for its effect on a kind of ritual.

5
Religious Drama in
—Medieval Europe———

In the early centuries of the Christian era, there is scanty evidence that the actor continued to exist. The theatres of the Roman Empire remained empty and crumbled away, except where they were taken over for the building of houses. The playwrights were no longer performed, although their works were sometimes imitated by those who wished to practise the reading and writing of Latin or, as schoolmasters, wished to teach others to do so.

Such references as there are to the players appear in legal and ecclesiastical documents and are not complimentary. The player is equated with the rogue, the vagabond, the beggar, the harlot and the thief. There is no doubt that there was some truth in these accusations. Equally, we must remember that the accusers were all ecclesiastics. Some of them were monks who had withdrawn from the wicked world in which the poor player was striving to survive. Others were concerned with the making and enforcement of law and order. Law and order, as they knew, was always at risk when large crowds gather—and was it not a habit of wandering players to gather large crowds about them?

Nowhere in the dramatic literature extant at the beginning of the Middle Ages was there any dramatization whatever of the rich literature of the Bible itself. It is strange that it never occurred to these learned men that they could create their own drama and teach and propagate Christianity. Centuries had to pass before this could happen. For the unlearned and for the pagans of the north, beyond the reaches of Christianity, entertainments of sorts persisted around the fires on the long winter evenings. It is likely also that the trade fairs, both large and small, would have attracted all kinds of performer. It is also very likely that some of these wandering entertainers would have travelled in troupes. Therefore it is likely that, even if they had no scripts, perhaps not even the ability to read, they would have improvised scenes however short that could be categorized as drama. (Here is the beginning of the famous Commedia dell' Arte, to be discussed later. See Chapter 6).

Much of the foregoing is, inevitably, conjecture but the frequent reference to *jongleurs,* in the sense of entertainers, justifying that this was a recognized and widespread profession. It is reasonable to suppose that even in areas that were officially Christian, the older religions concerned with nature worship still persisted and that their rituals found expression in dances and other performances. Here, the costumed player would have been continuing at work. Some of these performances, as we have seen, persist to this very day.

THE JESTER

Another interesting character whose origins are shrouded in mystery, but who is mentioned in documents of this time, is one of the prototype costumed players—the court jester. Whole books have been written about him but, from our point of view, perhaps his most important attribute was his costume. While other servants wore a livery, which indicated their allegiance to a certain master, he wore a livery that asserted his independence of his master and his allegiance to his craft. His status as fool gave him the right to speak the truth in and out of season. As Shakespeare made a philosopher remark, 'Invest me in my motley, give me leave to speak my mind.' It is obvious that not every jester of the Middle Ages was a Feste or even a Touchstone but they do seem to have maintained the tradition of storyteller, musician and wit all through the Dark Ages. They started to die out as the new companies of players arose in the sixteenth century.

Centuries passed but very little changed. The Church possessed buildings of increasing magnificence, capable of seating audiences of increasing size. Its priesthood was dressed increasingly richly. Its ritual provided opportunities for music and movement. It had a literature full of stories with theatrical potential but, unlike the great religions of the East, Christianity did not make use of these resources in the creation of great drama, until about the tenth century when the *tropes* appear.

THE TROPE

In those pre-Reformation days, the Church in Western Europe was one united body. A change made at Rome would spread rapidly through Italy to Spain, France, Germany and England. So it was with the liturgical *tropes*, that is to say additions and insertions into the Mass. These changes in the liturgy were made at the major festivals of Easter and Christmas. The process is very similar to the insertion of dialogue into the Greek dithyramb (see Chapter 3). Short dialogues in Latin, originally sung antiphonally between priest and choir, were extended by dramatization through impersonation of characters.

At the Easter ceremony one or more priests, dressed in white to represent angels, confronted three other priests dressed in robes to represent women. They had a dialogue in Latin, framed as question and answer.

'Whom do you seek, O Christian women?'
'Jesus of Nazareth, who was crucified, O Heavenly Ones.'
'He is not here. He has arisen from the sepulchre. Go and announce that He has arisen.'

This is not only a pleasing scene but it is dramatic, in the sense that there is impersonation, dialogue and action. This simple dramatization, usually referred to as the *Quem Queraetis* (Whom seek ye?) from its two initial Latin words, was but the beginning. It becomes obvious that similar treatment could be applied to whole sections of the Testament.

At first other episodes in the Gospels were dramatized in the same simple way; the performers were always priests and choristers; the language was Latin and the performance was kept in the chancel, that is to say, inside the priests' part of the church.

Next came the introduction of stage properties and a lengthening and elaboration of the story so that the whole church had to be used, both Nave and Chancel. The congregation became more involved. Different parts of the church became allocated to the performance of different parts of the story. A connection was established between time and place, so that from Bethlehem via Galilee to Gethsemane and Calvary became a logical progression. The simple robes used in the *Quem Queraetis* became replaced with more elaborate costumes. Characters began to carry attributes to make them readily recognizable. (St Peter had his keys in his belt, for instance). The dialogue, although remaining in Latin, was no longer strictly bound by the words of the Bible itself. The actors began to realize the possibilities of improvisation. For instance, there was a scene which was introduced quite early and became traditional in which the three Marys paused on their way so they could purchase spice. The stallholder became a comic character and his stall an obligatory addition to the setting. The very absence of authorized dialogue in the Bible for such a character gave scope, not to say licence, for comedy which was, no doubt, freely taken by the younger priests or more daring choristers. Such a scene in broad comic mime would appeal instantly to a lay audience which had no Latin. This lack of Latin on the part of the majority of the congregation precipitated the next great development.

The priesthood must have felt that it was a pity that so many of their flock were failing to understand the dialogue and action, so they must have been in favour of translating the plays into the vernacular. Strangely enough, it was this move towards popularization that led to secularization. We tend to forget how downright boring it may have been to live in the Middle Ages. The common people, especially, must have been starved of music, colour and public fun. When the plays were first translated, and became accessible through vernacular performances, the largest churches became so crammed with eager congregations that the authorities had to think carefully about the function of drama in the church. It must have seemed that what was, after all, simply a part of the rituals of the church was being expanded to swamp the whole. So it became necessary to move the performance out of the church into an area in front of the great West Door. (The porch may well have become a sort of tiring-house or dressing room).

Religious drama in Western Europe continued to develop from the tenth to the fifteenth centuries and its development prepared the way for the rise of professionalism in the Western theatre. The process was

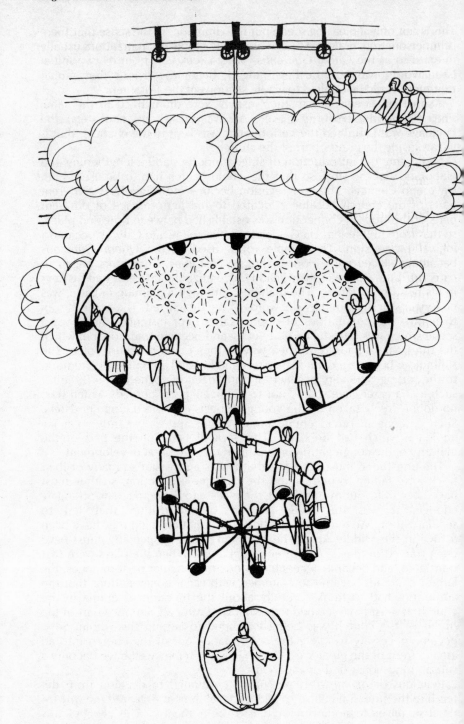

complex, so the following paragraphs are an attempt to provide a framework within which some particular examples may be considered.

The move away from giving performances inside the church building began in the twelfth century but it took place at different times in different countries. Sometimes it was as late as the fifteenth century and in some countries, such as Spain, the plays never entirely ceased from being performed inside the church.

Plays of this period are usually classified into four types, as follows:

1   *The liturgical play:* a drama derived from a *trope,* (see above) and developed at length. Unlike the other types of play listed here, which are always in the vernacular, the liturgical play is always in Latin.

2   *The mystery play:* a Bible history play, based on stories drawn from both Old and New Testaments. These were also produced in Spain, Italy, Germany and France.

3   *The miracle play:* a term partly synonymous with the mystery play but including stories not in the Bible, such as lives of the saints, etc.

4   *The morality play:* later than the others, not appearing until the fifteenth century. The characters are abstractions of virtues and vices. Obvious examples are in *Everyman,* translated into English in 1495 from the Dutch. There is also a German version. *The Castle of Perseverance* (see below) was a typical morality of the kind being professionally produced by the companies of travelling players. The professionals seem to have left the mystery and miracle plays to the societies and guilds in order to concentrate on moralities.

Performances can be classified according to *shape of presentation.* Some early productions kept to the long narrow shape suggested by the church interior, while others were in the round. Another distinction that could be made is between the *static* presentation and the *mobile.* Before looking at examples of these, one other general factor must be considered. In England and Germany, the craft guilds took over the control of the plays from the church. In Spain, France and Italy the organization was undertaken by the lay brotherhoods. Throughout Europe Corpus Christi day, a moveable feast early in the summer, was set aside as a holiday on which there could be religious processions and performances.

Against this general background, we can now consider some typical styles and shapes of presentation.

◀ *Reconstruction of the Machinery for Paradise as used in San Felice Church in Florence for the representation of the Annunciation during the fifteenth century. The whole gigantic machine was supported on a great beam set across the timbers of the church roof and contained no less than 20 children, dressed as angels and firmly strapped to the apparatus. From this 'paradise' descended an egg-like 'glory' from which stepped the actor playing the Archangel Gabriel. The reconstruction is based on a description by the artist Vasari and the machine itself was invented by the architect Filippo Brunelleschi*

THE MANSION

One early shape was long and narrow. This was due partly to the constraints of having to perform in a street or market place, but also to the habits of thought engendered in those leading actors who may have remembered seeing performances inside the church. For instance, at the east end of the church there was always the high altar, with its crucifix. It was natural, therefore, in setting scenes for a series of plays, to have the Crucifixion at the east end of the street and, beyond it, Heaven and the Last Judgement. Just as in the church performances places had been allocated around the walls for the Holy Sepulchre, the Pharisees, Galilee, and so on, similar spaces were allocated along the street and, just as in the church, Hell was situated as far from Heaven as possible, usually at the west end of the street. (Here is an example of compass-point symbolism. The Chinese did likewise, see Chapter 4.)

Varying terminology was used as the generic term for these places and the structures that were put on them. The commonest terms are those that can be translated as house or mansion although these are slightly misleading terms. It might be better to think of the structure as being more like a pavilion or a rather fancy stand at an exhibition, resembling a miniature stage decorated to suit the style of the scene to be played within it.

A very good, frequently illustrated, example is the Valenciennes passion play. This occurred rather late in the period and may represent a final flowering of this form. The illustrations show very clearly that, although the structures were temporary, they were artistically designed, strongly built and made to be taken apart and carefully stored between performances. Heaven was represented by an hexagonal pavilion, three sides of which were open and three draped; above it was a very large circular plaque depicting God seated at judgement with various figures standing around Him and angels flying around in a complete circle. Nazareth appears to be a simple gateway serving as no more than an entrance to a fenced off courtyard. The temple of Jerusalem and Herod's palace are much more elaborate structures reproducing a conglomeration of architectural features, as if the designer had had access to a master mason's pattern book. The celebrated Greek or Roman pillars and pediments, for instance, appear in front of Herod's palace, above Renaissance dungeons.

Moving downwards, away from Heaven, there is the Golden Gate and, in front of it, the sea of Galilee on which floated a ship. Beyond that is the *piece de résistance* of the medieval designer's skill—Hell itself. Entered by the great gaping mouth of a goggling monster, with sharp fangs silhouetted against a dull red glow, it was a sort of tower with hanging galleries and windows from which peeped monsters and devils of all sorts.

Heaven seems to have been nearly always set stage right and Hell stage left. (Right or left from the actors' point of view). Is this how the word for left—sinister—acquired its second meaning? In any case, it seems to be that evil is always more exciting to depict than good.

The space between the mansions was sometimes called the *platea* or place. This area had no particular location in the cycle of plays. It served to enable the audience to move from one mansion to another. Also the places in the story could be linked by members of the cast moving across the *platea*. For example, the demons could emerge from Hell and approach Paradise, threatening a few sinners on the way.

There does not seem to have been any special provision or limitation of space for the audience. Throughout the whole of this period we shall notice different forms of theatre arising to solve just this problem. One first step was to discontinue the practice of having the mansions on both sides of the street and to limit them, as at Valenciennes, to one side only. It is possible that privileged spectators may have had their own canopied stand, set in a commanding position, but even so they may not have seen as much as those who were prepared to stay at ground level and, literally, follow the action from place to place.

This form of setting in a straight line was more common on the Continent than in England. Here, the most common form was the pageant, which we shall discuss later. When an English performance was static, then it commonly took the form of the round.

THE MEDIEVAL ROUND

At this point in his history, the atavistic memory of the costumed player may have been slightly stirred. He may have had a feeling of having been here before. Some of the circles used for the performance of Christian plays had been Roman amphitheatres.

In England, it is necessary to distinguish between the amateur Cornish plays and the much larger, more elaborate professional performance such as *The Castle of Perseverance*. The Cornish plays, probably copied from Brittany, were set in amphitheatres dug out of open fields to a width of 30 to 40 feet. A writer in 1602 says: 'The country people flock from all sides...for they have therein devils and devices to delight the eye and ear'. The dialogue is full of local allusions. For instance, King Solomon appears very familiar with the names of villages around Lostwithiel. Some authorities say that the actors did not memorize their parts but were accompanied by a prompter who whispered their lines to them. In fact, it is more likely that this prompter was a Master of Ceremonies who intoned the whole play to set the pace and the rhythm. In any case, the title of prompter was used in those days in a way analogous to the modern stage manager or even producer. The practice certainly continues in many parts of Europe today.

Other medieval rounds were larger than those in Cornwall. Some of them persist to this day. Dimensions of 126 feet and over 200 feet have been quoted for them. The evidence, although limited, is considerably detailed. *The Castle of Perseverence* is taken as being particularly typical. There is a plan of the staging on a manuscript of the play itself which was written in about 1425.

The players were not guild-amateurs but full time professionals, so one of their major problems was to make sure that every member of the audience would have to pay before he could get in to see the show. The answer was obvious. There was one way in only and this was near to the tent used by the players as a dressing room so that any one of them, off duty, could act as box office keeper. Having paid him, members of the public passed across a bridge over a moat and came immediately into the acting area. The architectural model was that of the circular moated castle with earthworks on the inside made from the earth dug out of the ditch which made the moat. In the centre of the circular arena was erected the wooden tower which became the Castle of Perseverance itself, raised on stilt-like legs so that it did not obstruct the view too much, but provided a high vantage point to be used by actors at climactic moments.

Round the edge of the circle were the mansions, set always at certain points of the compass. God had His scaffold in the East, the scaffold for the World stood to the West, for the Devil in the North, for the Flesh in the South and for Covetousness in the North East. The audience entered between the world and the flesh. They spread themselves around, following the action from scaffold to scaffold but, in order to prevent them from getting in the way of the action in the 'place' between the scaffolds, there driven around by stewards, called stytlers, who drove the crowd very much like a stockman driving his sheep.

It is worth pausing to consider the effects of the circular shape upon the art of theatre. Size itself is a critical factor. If the play is to be a small one with a simple plot line and few actors, as in the case of the Marshfield Mumming Play (see Chapter 2), then they themselves can clear enough space in a crowd that has already assembled. Performances on a larger scale, with many more actors and a longer and more complex storyline, created different problems. For economic reasons alone, a large audience would be absolutely necessary but to keep it interested in the story would require very careful marshalling, as we have seen. It is worth noting that a production using a technique similar to this was staged in Paris and at the Round House, London, in the 1970s. It told the story of the French Revolution and purported to take place in a great public park where there were various side shows mounted where instalments of the story took place. There was also, in 1980, a production of *Hamlet* in which the audience followed the action about the theatre, and in the same year, various so-called promenade performances at the National Theatre.

To return to the Middle Ages, it is obvious that professional players would not always dig ditches or build ramparts. It is fairly safe to deduce that they may have simply built circular fences. There is a very famous miniature frequently reproduced (see Bibliography), representing a performance of *The Martyrdom of St Apollonia* which shows booths surrounding a central open space where the saint, apparently played by a woman, is being realistically tortured. The booths are occupied—one by angels, one by devils and one by trumpeters—but we do not know whether the occupants of the other booths depicted are privileged spectators or more performers. We do not know whether the picture represents a performance set in a line as at Valenciennes or, as is more likely, the artist has merely shown us one half of the round. There is a large crowd in the background and, presumably, if they were to see everything they would have had to be 'stytled' around.

From this example it is a logical step to simply erecting a circular open tent. This calls to mind both the Roman amphitheatre and the contemporary touring circus. 'Theatre without theatre' continues.

SECULARIZATION AND THE RISE OF PROFESSIONALISM

We should bear in mind, however, that the costumed player in England was usually an amateur, although some received fees. He spent the working hours at his craft and his leisure in preparing and performing. Nonetheless he was a skilful amateur, eager and willing to learn from professionals about him and, when he finally disappeared from the scene, he left a body of knowledge and a tradition of expertise which was useful to those who followed him.

We must remember that there was a period of overlap. For instance it would have been possible for Shakespeare to have seen a guild performance. There is internal evidence in the works of other Elizabethan writers, such as Marlowe, of familiarity with the style of the mystery and morality play. This style, like most artistic styles, arose from the need to solve practical problems.

When the city guilds took over the business of performing the mystery and miracle plays, it was logical for them to share out the Bible stories between them. Some very appropriate choices seem to have been made, with the carpenters set the building of Noah's Ark and the fishmongers in the story of Jonah and the Whale. Performances were usually on a holiday at a time of year when fine weather might be expected, such as at Whitsun or the Feast of Corpus Christi. In England, we have records of whole cycles of mystery plays so allocated, surviving in the archives of towns and cities such as York, Chester, Wakefield and others. In essence the plays follow the Bible story closely but there are often additional characters such as Mrs Noah's drinking companions, and a sheepstealer added to the Nativity story, providing opportunities for earthy comedy. It is possible that the devils had a general function rather like that of the continuity entry-clowns in a modern circus.

PAGEANT CARTS

If all the larger and more influential guilds were to take part, there must have been up to a dozen performances to get through in one day. (Some authorities say that the average was eight.) This would have been a long programme and the audience would have been virtually the entire population of the town with additions from the surrounding villages.

The mystery plays had outgrown the church centuries beforehand and there would be no open space within the city walls large enough to contain all the actors and audience at the same time. The solution was obvious to the guildsmen who were well used to watching, and taking part in, royal progressions and civic processions through the town. They made their mansions mobile by setting them on wheels so that each scene in the total play was its own little theatre. (It is difficult to say whether the processions preceded or followed the pageant-wagon. Historically it is most likely that they were simultaneous, but the procession survived after the mobile mystery play had died out.)

To take one example from Norwich in 1565, the grocers' pageant was 'a howse of waynskotte paynted and buylded on a cart with fowre whelys'. It would have been easy enough to allocate areas of the town for each guild to start from a timetable by which they changed places. The change-over time would be an interval for refreshments. In this way the audience is spread throughout the town in manageable numbers.

That, at least, is the generally accepted notion but, when we consider the dimensions of these wagons, we must pause for further thought. According to Wickham (see Bibliography), a complete pageant would have been made up from two carts, each 15 feet wide and 30 feet long. One of these had the mansion mounted on it with a tiring house behind it, or possibly below it. The other cart remained empty but was drawn in front of the mansion to make a performance platform. When we consider the narrowness and the curvature of many a medieval street, even a main thoroughfare, then this accepted idea must need modification. How, for instance, could the movement of these carts be so arranged as to avoid traffic jams when they passed each other? Perhaps there was no second cart, but the actors used the front of the pageant-wagon and street level as well. Perhaps the carts were smaller than most authorities say they were. There is no clear documentation of English pageants but their Spanish equivalent, the *nutos,* definitely used two carts.

THE GUILDMAN PLAYER

What, then, were the resources of the guildman-player? His script would have been written down, probably by a priest, choir-master or school master some years back and he would have learned the part as much by watching and listening to his predecessor as in reading and memorizing. The records are rich in lists of fine costumes which were guild property and carefully preserved. These were sometimes both beautiful and ingenious. His apprenticeship as an actor may well have coincided with his apprenticeship in his craft and, in an all-male organization, it may well have fallen to him as an apprentice to play women's parts, although the character female roles were usually taken by master actors.

In that he received fees for playing, he was not entirely amateur. The records show entries such as 'three shillings and four pence for playing God'. His most important attributes were his appearance and his voice. Some parts were traditionally played by tall, fat or lean men, for instance.

All actors needed powerful voices to project and sustain the long lines of narrative verse. Some characters were played in a traditional style. Herod, for instance, was expected to go into a terrifying rage when he heard of the flight into Egypt. Music appears to be ancillary to the drama but there is at least one example of a carol originally being composed as part of the nativity section of a miracle cycle.

We must now once more look beyond the theatre to see what was happening in the world at large during the sixteenth century. This was the time when the miracle and mystery plays were at their best in England but by 1590 they had virtually disappeared. It was the fully professional player who came into the ascendant and had a legal monopoly of performance. For a full understanding of the complex reasons for this, we refer the reader to Professor Wickham's series of books, *Early English Stages*, Volume II Part I, but we shall endeavour to summarize the process.

During the entire period that we call the Middle Ages and for the most part persisting into the period that we call the Renaissance, there were several distinct groups of people who carried on the arts of theatre in England in a number of different ways for different purposes. First of all, there was the continuing group of professional players. These were, as it were, the descendants of the *jongleurs*. The quality of their talent varied and they depended on the goodwill of holiday crowds or, later, on the patronage of the wealthy. It is worth noting here, for the benefit of those who have grown up since the acceptance of the principle of the Welfare State, that a totally independent professional group would literally face starvation when times were bad. So their alternatives were in beggary, theft or prostitution—just the three crimes of which the actor was frequently accused. Nevertheless, by the end of the century, many professional players were under the protection of the high aristocracy and of the Crown itself.

The new Grammar Schools had begun the long tradition in England of schoolmaster-playwright and schoolmaster-producer. Some of the schoolboys were to become professional players as apprentices. Others went on to the universities, continued their study of the classics and came back as playwrights perhaps, or at least patrons of theatre.

One major influence on the theatre was the dissolution of the monasteries. This meant that quite suddenly the previously sheltered monks found themselves simultaneously homeless and unemployed. Some of these may have joined professional companies and they may even have added a modicum of learning to some of the more bedraggled troupes.

There was also, in the growing cities, a general pattern of civic display and entertainment. This was parallel to, and sometimes in rivalry with, the royal pageantry and progressions. Such events frequently took the form of a grand procession generally devised around a theme by a master designer to a script written by a poet. In the early seventeenth century Ben Jonson, John Webster and John Middleton were all involved in this kind of work for the City of London. Later still Jonson, with Inigo Jones as designer, developed this form of entertainment into the court masque (see Chapter 7).

We must not forget two other groups who were practising a kind of theatre in markedly different circumstances. Here and there, throughout the countryside away from highways, ancient pre-Christian customs were still being celebrated in the dark of the moon or boldly in plain sunlight. These would continue to persist no matter what the clergy said. Their dramas were not yet documented, but then, how could we expect them to be? On the other hand, in the halls of the great houses, and sometimes on their lawns or in their knot gardens, the young people of the new Protestant aristocracy continued a kind of theatre based on the ritual of the courts of love and chivalry.

POLITICS AND THE PLAYER

There still remains the outstanding question as to why it was that miracle, mystery and morality plays faded away and were replaced by secular plays performed by professionals inside the new theatres. To oversimplify slightly, we would suggest the reasons lie in the politics of the time. The Tudors were totalitarian monarchs. They did not object to theatre but wanted a theatre that would be directly under their control. Through the Revels Office, they instituted a censorship which did not forbid discussion of matters of public interest, but laid down rules deciding what could be discussed and how it could be discussed.

The playwrights became important. Their scripts were read in the Revels Office, not merely to search them for obvious treason or impropriety, but to see if they were hinting at important matters 'between the lines'. It became necessary to control the writer by licensing the company of players who were to perform his work. This was done by means of a legal device by which all actors were the liveried servants of some great landowner. This meant that those who held no licence could no longer perform in public and receive fees for it. The new and reformed Church of England neither asked for, nor was likely to receive, a performing licence. The city Guilds also received no licence so, in the upshot, there was a monopoly established for the new kind of professional player, such as Shakespeare, Burbage and Alleyn whose work we shall be considering later on.

Thus the Renaissance came to the English theatre, but brought the Reformation with it. It is the unlicenced, unprotected player who bears the continual brunt of the attacks from the Puritans whenever they are in power, and even the companies favoured by the Court find difficulty in establishing themselves inside the city of London. (It is, perhaps, not altogether a coincidence that the British National Theatre in London stands midway between royal Westminster and the mercantile City but on the South Bank of the river).

Second Interlude

ABOUT INTERLUDES

Most historians of theatre devote most space to the discussion of great public events, the performances of religious cycles, and to the emergence of the national theatres of the world. While there is reason for this, it is not merely unfair but misleading to overlook the smaller, more private theatre of friendly entertainment. After all, mankind cannot be serious, noble and elevated all the time. He must have the chance to relax and enjoy himself.

We have given some indication of how professionalism came about by showing how the company player replaced the guild player. If we wish to understand how it was that Elizabethan drama came to replace the guild play then we must consider, briefly, the rise of the Interlude. This form of entertainment arose in Renaissance Italy and spread through Western Europe. It was a dramatic entertainment given during a banquet, especially during the intervals between the courses. The best modern parallel to the Interlude is the short sketch in cabaret or on television, involving perhaps a comedian and one or two assistants.

Professional authors and actors found that it was worth their while to provide such entertainment. John Heywood was well known as a writer of interludes as early as 1520. Henry VII employed professionals to provide such entertainment at the wedding festivities for his daughter. Such an event was important in the history of English theatre, in that it brought the players into contact with the Court. They remained the servants of the Crown after the Interlude had been replaced by the longer play.

Playing to a distinguished audience in a banqueting hall created problems. In solving these, the players helped to lay the foundations of the Elizabethan theatre.

6
The Shape of the Stage

THE BOOTH

In the hundred years from 1560 to 1660, theatre in England passed through a series of changes which are both extraordinary and unique in the history of the art. There are four stages in this process, as follows: First, the decline of the guild players and the rise of the new professionals as already described. Second, the erection of new kinds of purpose-built public playhouses in the Elizabethan style from 1576 onward. Third, the growing pressure against theatres from the extreme Protestants, increasing up to the English Civil War and culminating in the closure of theatres in England in 1642. Fourth, the Restoration of the monarchy (1660) under Charles II and the building of public playhouses very different from the Elizabethan. Both the Elizabethan and Restoration playhouses will be discussed later.

Once again, we must point out that these historical periods tend to overlap. While it is true that when Charles first came back from exile he brought continental ideas with him, some of those ideas had already been mooted here in England. For example there had been roofed playhouses as early as 1605.

In the next few chapters we shall discuss both periods in some detail but, before we do so, we intend to step back a little to look for the origins of the key features of the two different kinds of playhouse, especially the stage itself. We listed the stage, together with place and background as the external resources of the costumed player (see Chapter 1). In the early phases of theatre art, the place is simply any empty space that the player creates between himself and his audience. His stage is the ground he walks on. These may have their own natural advantages. A mound becomes a natural platform; the dawn sky or the edge of a forest becomes a natural background.

Anyone who has performed in street theatre, or by the seaside, or in front of really impressive scenery knows how distracting such natural backgrounds can become. The actor is aware that his audience may have a greater interest in what is going on behind him than in his performance. Had he been wise with the cunning of his craft, the actor would have set up some sort of simple screen to mask the background. This would have had a twofold purpose. It would have cut the audience off from the distraction, and it would also create a new area of hidden mystery which

Booth stage as seen in many European paintings but also in use world wide

would excite their curiosity. They would want to know what was hidden behind the screen, so when the actor appears, preferably into the centre of his stage through a slit in the screen, he arrives as a person coming from a hidden world. This is one reason why actors love to enter from up-stage centre. Inevitably, they bring with them the magic and mystery of the theatre.

Obviously, it is possible to make an entrance without having a background to come through or round and many players do this very successfully but the entrance can never be so clearcut, neither can the exit. In short, the audience are never *quite* sure when the performance has started and when it is over. Entrance and exit are not only the boundaries but part of the essence of the actor's art. It is a tremendous help to him to have ways in and ways out. Once he has them he may develop an infinite number of uses for them.

Again, it is possible for a highly skilled actor to dominate his audience from ground level, but for economy of effort (and professionalism rests upon such economy) it is much better if he is raised above them. More important than this, the actor must be seen by every member of his audience. *Stage sight lines* should be the guide lines for theatre planning.

Booth stage set in inn yard

We have seen how very early in the history of the theatre a dressing room became, after stage and background, the next essential. It must be as near to the stage as possible. The problem was solved by the Greeks by making the dressing room (*skena*) the background to the stage. Though, it could also be, as in some pageant-wagons, underneath the raised stage. The player is now beginning to make a working place for himself and home for his personal resources such as his mask, costume and musical instruments. His properties and his stage furniture will also need adjacent storage. At first, perhaps, dressing room and store could be the same place but, as companies grew and the performances became more elaborate, separate accommodation was necessary. For instance the Elizabethans solved the problem with the dressing room behind the stage and the property store below it.

When we look back over the last few paragraphs, it becomes obvious that we are in the process of listing the requirements for an efficient professional theatre. Dr Southern lists these requirements in his book and adds two others. One of these is a means of acquiring a higher level on the stage. Once the actor has been raised up above his audience, he can exploit the dramatic possibilities of being raised up over another actor. This effect can be achieved very simply by making an upper window in the background and hiding a ladder behind the scene. The dramatic possibilities are infinite. Shakespeare found a number of ways of using the 'above'. Also, if the construction is to be used by professionals in competition with other attractions, then it must be decorated in some way to make it pleasing and attractive and, finally, if it is to be taken around for fairs and feast days, it must be readily portable. If it is to stay in one place, it must be weatherproof.

Dr Southern argues that these requirements were very well understood by the professional players of Europe and elsewhere and that, by the middle of the sixteenth century at least, they had solved the practical problems themselves by the creation of what he calls the *booth stage*. While some authorities would doubt the ability of the players to invent and construct such stages without the assistance of other specialists, such as architects and engineers, it seems commonsense to suppose that, since the players were the only people who understood their own problems, it is very likely that they were capable of finding their own solutions. Southern sets the date of 1542 in Western Europe for the emergence of the booth stage. We would guess at an earlier time. It may be more useful for us to think not in terms of dates and places but in terms of phases in the development of the theatre arts.

The booth stage marks the beginning of a phase of professionalism. As the professionals became more successful so that audiences came to them rather than vice versa, then the booth stage could be included within a permanent building. (As indeed it was in Shakespeare's time). We shall test our ideas about the booth stage by examining several different examples of its use by professional players. Our first example comes from Athens 24 centuries ago; the second from seventeenth-century Italy and

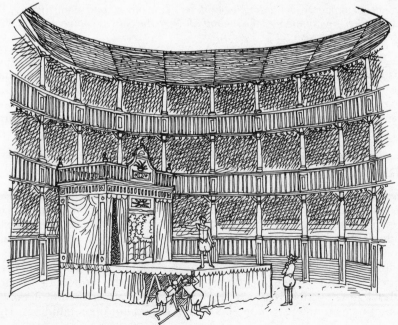

Booth stage set in bull/bear baiting arena

65

Later development from the simple booth set in the blood sport arena to the architectural environment of the second Globe in the early seventeenth-century Elizabethan playhouse.

the third from nineteenth-century China. This would appear to be a reasonably representative example of the threatre art in one particular phase of development, irrespective of particular chronology and geographical circumstances. It is true of all arts that a technique invented by craftsmen in one place in one era may be forgotten and subsequently reinvented elsewhere and much later in time.

PHYLAX

So it was with this kind of platform used for the performance of the *Phylax* (See Chapter 3), a form of mime play of the fourth century BC. Being essentially temporary structures, none of them survived to the time when scholars began to revive interest in Greek drama. Indeed, just because the only evidence was on vase-paintings rather than in massive temple-like theatres, some scholars even doubted that the Phylax ever existed. Nowadays, we are quite familiar with the notion of theatre without theatre, that is to say the idea that the art of theatre depends upon the costumed player and his resources and not upon buildings. The plays themselves seem to bridge the gap between Greek and Roman comedy. The stages on which they were performed seemed to incorporate features which bridge the gap between Greek and Roman theatre buildings. They were simple to make and to erect, consisting of tall posts which supported a wooden platform, the posts themselves being joined by wooden panels with ornamental patterns painted on them. These panels were pierced with a practical door and, later, windows.

COMMEDIA DELL'ARTE

Our next example comes from Italy and concerns one of the most interesting and exciting forms that theatre art has ever taken. Of all the styles of acting extant in Europe between the sixteenth and seventeenth centuries that of the Italian Commedia dell'Arte ranks equal with the English professional theatre, albeit in a markedly different way. (See also Chapter 4).

In many ways it is the direct opposite of the theatre of Shakespeare, Jonson and indeed any writer's theatre. Plot and language are of little importance. The actors worked to a scenario of a fairly trivial story of love and intrigue, improvising as they went along. They had no playwright to create great individual characters such as Falstaff or Hamlet. Each of the ten or twelve actors, for the whole of their careers, played one stock character only. This would appear to be a recipe for dreary buffoonery and not worthy of comparison with what was shown at, say, the Globe theatre but, for the art form to have survived for more than two hundred years and to have spread into France, Spain, England and even Russia, to remain popular on fairgrounds but also to be invited to the courts of kings, implies a high degree of professional skill.

There used to be a song entitled 'It ain't what you do, it's the way that you do it'. This could almost be the motto of the Commedia dell'Arte. The term dell'Arte itself can be translated as 'of the profession' and the players accepted very seriously the disciplines of their art. Usually they were born into one of the travelling family companies, and married from one into another. Both men and women took part. Women could and frequently did lead and manage their own companies. The children were set to learn dancing and acrobatics as soon as they could walk and frequently they kept their skills into advanced old age. It is said of one actor that at the age of 83 he could still kick high enough to knock his partner's hat off.

Every member of the company, as we have said, specialized in one or other of the great Commedia character parts. There were many of these, each with a distinctive costume and (for the men) mask. The most famous and enduring included Harlequin, the sly, witty, acrobatic servant, Columbina the pretty, graceful and unscrupulous maid-servant, Pantaloon, sometimes depicted as their employer, old, miserly and lecherous; the boastful and cowardly Captain; the polysyllabic but stupid Doctor and many others.

The names and characteristics persist to this day. These characters have appeared in puppet shows throughout the West. One, indeed, Polchinello, his name anglicized to Punch, had a puppet show all to himself. The Harlequinade of the English pantomime, the stylised make-up and business of the great French mimes from Dubureau to Marceau, the basic physical gags of the silent film comedy, all owe their origins to the precision and dedication of these master craftsmen of the Commedia dell'Arte. All are part of the great *jongleur* tradition of non-literary theatre. The plot was simply a device to display the skills of the performers in a series of *lazzi*. This was the name given to the interpolated business or dialogue. This could vary from a highspeed series of pratfalls, through sophisticated and subtle mime to ornate and fanciful dialogue.

Their skills were so universally acclaimed as to attract the attention of English professionals, notably Kemp, one of the leading comedians of the Globe. He not only went to France to work with the Commedia and to learn from them, but he later set up his own company known as the English Comedians which toured very successfully in Germany. Even when the Commedia was in decline, in the eighteenth century, the great English actor, Garrick, was so impressed by the acting of one Carlin Bertinazzi that he is reported as having explained 'His very back has character and expression!'

In their early travelling days the Commedia companies would have used what was fundamentally the booth type of stage. Early drawings show them working on high scaffolds in two squares, against simple backgrounds, usually unpainted. Later, there is a rough sketch of a perspective street. Sometimes sections of the curtain are brought forward to give relief to the background. A later development was to have two small houses on opposite sides of the stage, each provided with a practical door and window above. There is a very famous illustration of such a scene which depicts an attempted elopement, with a character being drenched with water from one of the windows. (The Commedia called for rapid and sometimes surprising entrances and exits. Such a set would enable them to achieve a whole variety of comic *lazzi*, all around the simple idea of entrance and exit.)

Later still, in about the 1660s and into the eighteenth century when they had moved into the indoor theatres, they begin to use elaborate and detailed perspective street scenes, although their art has little to do with the theatre of illusion.

In the nineteenth-century pantomime, when the Commedia itself was dead, the Harlequin figure remained, frequently appearing in front of a street scene, but this might well have trap doors built into it, not only in the stone floor, but into the scenery itself so that Harlequin could appear and disappear with bewildering rapidity, thus reasserting the triumph of sheer entertainment skill over a certain kind of pseudo-realism.

It is worth pausing here to ask an important question. What did the Commedia dell'Arte gain by moving into permanent roofed playhouses with elaborate scenery? Was their art improved by it? Surely the answer is that the success or otherwise of the performances depended entirely upon the skill of the players and architecture could add little or nothing.

PEKIN OPERA

Let us now draw a parallel from a place and time distant from the Commedia but, in our terminology, in the same phase of artistic development. We refer to the Chinese classical theatre especially as it was in the nineteenth and twentieth centuries at the Pekin Opera, until it was badly disrupted by the Maoist Cultural Revolution. At first sight, it is markedly different from the Commedia but, on closer examination, it is remarkably similar.

Mask and stylized costume in the one are reflected by stylized make-up and costume in the other. Chinese and Italian audiences alike were not interested in plot or subtle characterization but took delight in the sheer skill of the performers. Both Chinese and Italian were accomplished acrobats trained up from infancy and equally singers, dancers, actors and mimes. The Italian *lazzi* had their counterpart in even more elaborately sustained bravura set-pieces. Incidents in the main story are expanded into quite lengthy sequences such as 'the fight in the dark'. In this, two acrobatic dancers working on a fully lit stage mime and tumble so precisely that we are convinced that they cannot see each other. But for the comedy, the tension of a series of apparently accidental hairsbreadth escapes is almost unbearable. There are no props except the swords, which have real cutting edges to them, and the only scenery is a table, which the actors use as a sort of vaulting horse.

In another famous sequence, a lady has to be ferried across a river. Again, the incident is expanded. The ferryman is old, absent-minded, so that he forgets to untie the raft before he can punt it out into the stream. There is a strong current in the river; the raft bobs up and down and swings as it crosses the stream; the young lady is nervous but maintains her dignity. Yet this takes place on a bare stage. There is no river, no raft. The only prop is the ferryman's pole. The illusion created is perfect.

The stage itself was no more than yet another example of the booth stage, consisting of a square platform, a roof above it supported on columns and two doors in the back wall. Conventionally, entrances were made stage right and exits stage left. The audience was on three sides and the dressing room was behind the scene.

We could multiply examples of this phase of theatre, drawing examples from other times and places but we will now return to the question we raised about the Commedia and ask it about the Chinese. Once again, how much would the actors have gained by being given more architectural resources? To answer this question we must consider the *basic conventions*. The art of the actor playing in *realistic drama*, whether it be a gangster movie or one of the plays of Ibsen, must give the appearance of reality. He must be seen against a background which imitates the supposed reality as closely as possible, to the point where the spectator will willingly accept the illusion with no qualms at all. Yet it is a fact that most theatre is written and played in a non-naturalistic convention. This includes, besides the example given above, all the plays of Shakespeare and his contemporaries and much that has been written since.

Non-realistic theatre works well on the booth stage and in theatres derived from the booth stage; realistic theatre needs a different kind of stage and, therefore, a different kind of theatre. When Laurence Olivier produced *Henry V* on film, he inadvertently illustrated differences in convention. The film began and ended with a representation of a performance inside an Elizabethan theatre. The main part of the film used location, especially for battle scenes. Yet the play begins with a prologue asking the audience to use their imaginations to suppose that 'within this wooden O' there could exist the 'two mighty monarchies' of England and France.

Other conventions changed. While after the Restoration some writers maintained the Elizabethan tradition of verse drama, others aimed to reproduce more naturalistic prose conversation. From this it was but a short step for them to demand naturalistic settings, so the playhouse had to be designed to make this possible. This is one partial explanation as to the changing shape of the theatre in the period from 1560 to 1660 in England.

With this in mind, let us examine more closely the process by which the booth stage developed, in England, into the kind of building that we think of as being the 'typical Elizabethan playhouse'. (We shall discover that, unfortunately, there is no typical Elizabethan theatre and that many illustrations of performances at the Globe are more conjectural than historical).

7
The Elizabethan
—Playhouse————————

The grand high summer of Elizabethan theatre begins, as it were, in a thick mist. Which clears fitfully so that we can see dim shapes of noble buildings and great men. Sometimes the mist clears long enough for us to know what took place and who took part; at other times it swirls tantalizingly back so that the scene becomes dim and scholars begin to argue about precisely what it is they think they see.

Setting aside the private theatres and the Court for later consideration, we will now pay attention to the eight public theatres that existed in London during this period. They were, in chronological order, The Theatre in Shoreditch, 1576; The Curtain, also in Shoreditch, 1576 or 1577; The Rose, Bankside, about 1587; The Swan, also Bankside 1595; The Globe, Shakespeare's Theatre, 1598 to 99, built on Bankside with timbers from the demolished Theatre in Shoreditch; The Fortune Theatre in Cripplegate, 1600, about the same time as The Red Bull in Clerkenwell, and in 1614 The Hope was also built on Bankside, as a mixture of playhouse and bear-baiting house.

These theatres were built mainly of timber and thatch so they were in constant fire hazard. The Globe itself was burnt down in 1613 when, it is said, the firing of a canon as part of the play of *Henry VIII* set fire to the roof. This famous theatre reopened in 1614 and was pulled down in 1644 after the closure of all English theatres in 1642. The site is very near that of the present British National Theatre on South Bank. Our knowledge of these theatres is based upon the builders' contracts for two of them (The Fortune and The Hope) and a sketch of The Swan made by a Dutch visitor named de Witt. There is indirect evidence in legal documents and accounts of performances, etc. However, the following example may give warning to the scholar of the pitfalls that await him, even when dealing with contemporary evidence.

An artist and engraver called Hollar made a panoramic view of London in Stuart times depicting two buildings standing near each other on the South Bank. One is labelled 'The Globe'; the other, 'Beare Bayting h'. (Bear Baiting house). In fact, all other evidence points to the fact that the name plates for the two buildings should have been reversed! The bear baiting house was also The Hope theatre, as we have already said.

Before we look more closely at the buildings and the great men who used them let us give attention to the men who built them and their reasons for so doing. We tend to think of the Elizabethan age, quite rightly, as the age of Shakespeare and his fellow-playwrights but we must never overlook the fact that these men would never have achieved immortality if it were not for the fact that, behind them, there were some very shrewd business men who seized a chance to make a profit.

GAMEHOUSES

The professional Interluders (see Chapter 6 page 61) who belonged to the liveried companies of players soon realized that their skill had a market value. They began to take their more successful items out of the banqueting halls and to show them to the public wherever they could. Any place in which they could erect a booth stage and control the entrance of the audience was suited to their purpose. (It is worth mentioning here that many scholars nowadays reject the idea that the inn yard is in any way ancestor to the Elizabethan playhouse. While it is likely that the players used inn yards, they did not do so exclusively. Furthermore the inn yards were usually rectangular or square whereas most Elizabethan play houses are polygonal and tending to the circular.) In any case, not only would there have been a fair amount of unused open land quite near to the heart of the city, but there did exist buildings and open-air fenced arenas which were known as game houses. These were available to be leased by anyone for public entertainment of all sorts, including not only plays, but what we should now call sporting events including wrestling, bull-baiting and bear-baiting. A modern analogy might be something like the Albert Hall, in London, where one can see boxing and a symphony concert on successive nights.

This multi-purpose gaming area remained the model chosen by the adventurous but cautious speculators who built the first theatres in England to be so called. They were adventurous in that they thought there was money in plays so they had a booth stage included in the contracts but, in case the plays lost money, the booth stage, being portable and not part of the structure of the building, could be removed and the room made ready for bear- and bull-baiting.

THE THEATRE: 1576

In fact, the first step in the creation of the Elizabethan theatre was to take a booth stage and set it up inside a gaming house. The first of these great speculators was *James Burbage (c 1530–1597)*. He had begun as a carpenter but became a professional actor relatively late in life at the age of about 40. In 1576 he combined the skills and knowledge of both crafts in the building of The Theatre in Shoreditch. (Very recent research, published in 1980, under the editorship of Herbert Berry—see Bibliography—suggests that this building was not, as everybody supposes, the first English playhouse of its kind. Calais was still English territory in 1520 Henry VIII caused a building very similar to The Theatre to be erected there for the entertainment of the Emperor. The same piece of research also suggests that, since sight-lines for baiting pits are notably different from those required for a theatre, we may have over-simplified the development of the playhouse.)

However, Burbage's Theatre was a great success and success brought imitation and The Curtain Theatre was opened in the same part of London within a year. The name was taken from the place where it was built, Curtain Close, Finsbury and, of course, has nothing whatever to do with the idea of a front curtain. This device was not to be used in English theatres until nearly a hundred years later. Although overshadowed by the glamour of The Globe, The Curtain had a long and distinguished history. The Chamberlain's Men appeared there and it is said that Shakespeare acted there in one of Ben Jonson's comedies. The Burbage family had connections, financial as well as artistic, with both theatres. The Theatre itself stayed open for twenty years and successfully overcame opposition from rival impresarios offering great variety of non-dramatic entertainment.

James Burbage had two sons. One, called Cuthbert, remained a businessman. Following litigation about the lease on The Theatre, he dismantled it and had it transported over the river to Bankside where it was re-erected and named The Globe. Here Cuthbert's brother, *Richard (c. 1567–1619)* became famous as the first great English actor. Unlike his father, he started acting while still in his teens and became leader of the Chamberlain's Men in 1594. He was the first actor to play King Lear, Hamlet and many other Shakespearian leads but also appeared in the works of Jonson and Webster. Cuthbert, like his father before him, kept a foot in both camps in that, although he was a builder and businessman, he also seems to have been an impresario of a sort.

The Burbage family had rivals. The most successful of these was *Edward Alleyn (1566–1626)*, an actor who created most of the great leading roles in the plays of Christopher Marlowe. It may well be that his style was more suited to the theatrical grandeur of Tamberlaine than it would have been to the subtleties of Hamlet. It is very likely that his performances at The Rose were sometimes parodied at The Globe. His father-in-law, *Richard Henslowe (died in 1616)* was probably the most financially successful of all the Elizabethan impresarios. He owned three theatres, The Fortune, The Hope and The Rose.

The Alleyn-Henslowe companies make an interesting contrast with the Burbage-Shakespeare company. The Chamberlain's Men were joint owners of The Globe and worked on a system based upon shareholding. (Some shares were larger than others and it is likely that the Burbage family did undertake some ventures independently but by and large the association was more like a co-operative than a capitalist enterprise.)

Henslowe, on the other hand, was sole owner of his theatres and kept actors and playwrights under contract to him. The repertory depended on his somewhat arbitrary choice but, worse than that, he seems to have been guilty of sharp practices by the use of which both actors and writers were continually in his debt. However, we must be grateful to him for leaving his business documents to Alleyn who bequeathed them to Dulwich College, which he founded. From these papers we learn much about the organization of the theatres of the time. It is obvious that theatre had quite suddenly become big business. Plays were popular with everyone, from courtier to apprentice, everyone or nearly everyone; we will consider the exceptions later.

THE DEVELOPED BOOTH: THE ELIZABETHAN PLAYHOUSE

Once a member of the great majority who loved his theatre had paid his penny to pass the gatekeeper, what was he likely to see as he stepped inside and looked around? This is a question we must try to answer but with the utmost caution. Elizabethan playhouses were as much alike and as little alike as the theatres of London today. Certain features appear in more than one of them, but not necessarily in every one. Besides the evidence of the builders' contracts and the de Witt drawing there is a variety of secondary evidence. The plays themselves in the versions that we use today are frequently based upon stage managers' copies and therefore contain stage directions and other notes which give hints of the architecture of the theatres in which the plays were performed. They also give clues as to how certain effects were achieved and, what is more, give strong indication as to what effects a playwright could reasonably ask for. (Beheadings, appearances 'above', ghosts and devils and 'quaint devices to make a banquet vanish' are all examples that need to be thought out in terms of the real facilities if they are to be properly produced.)

The contracts for The Fortune and The Hope theatres make it clear that the buildings were expected to be solid, durable and of good workmanship. There is evidence in de Witt's notes with his sketch and in letters and diaries of the time that the playhouses of London gave an impression of 'great beauty'. They were brightly painted and sometimes the back of the stage was hung with a bright arras. The most common shape for the whole building was octagonal or circular with the centre open to the sky, making the shape that Shakespeare called 'this wooden O'. The stages were not necessarily an integral part of the fabric of the building. In those days you could not brief your builder to make you a theatre and expect that it would include a stage. The stage had to be a specified item. (We must remember that some playhouses were still 'playhouses' or 'gamehouses' in the old sense of the word and sometimes reverted to bear-baiting. The Hope may have done this regularly and, in consequence, had a non-permanent wooden trestle stage.)

The dimensions of the stage would be of the order of 40 feet wide and up to about 30 feet deep. Judging by de Witt's sketch, the stage he was drawing was like what we should now call a thrust stage with the audience on three sides.

There seems to be no doubt that it was a custom for what were called the sixpenny gallants to sit upon the stage itself. (They do not seem to have been officially banished until the time of Charles II in a proclamation of 1673. No doubt they 'were being eased out before that.)

We must not forget these stoolholders when visualizing any Elizabethan performance. If they were present in any numbers, then they must have reduced the available acting space by perhaps 20 square feet or more. The stage floor could have been up to six feet above the ground level and, if so, then safety considerations suggest that it may well have been surrounded by a railing. Those were rather rowdy times and for an actor, or a sixpenny gallant, to fall six feet might have been somewhat dangerous.

We have said that the audience surrounded the stage on three sides and most authorities agree but there is some evidence, particularly the de Witt sketch, to suggest that they could have been on all four sides, that is to say behind the stage as well. Around the walls were galleries, reached by staircases from ground level by those who paid the extra to go upstairs and sit down. There were two and sometimes three of these ranging round the entire auditorium, with the upper storey roofed in thatch. Tiles were used later. The groundlings remained standing in the open air. It is no exaggeration to say that without them Elizabethan theatre could not have worked, in the sense of transmission of power from actor to audience. The groundlings were nearest to the stage, most ready and willing to react, easily bored perhaps, but most appreciative when pleased. When theatres were re-built, so that the sixpenny gallants occupied the front rows and the groundlings were sent up to the gallery, something was lost.

The stage itself, or at least most of it, would be protected from the elements by an awning or penthouse roof supported upon pillars. The underside of this canopy was frequently decorated by a representation, sometimes quite elaborate, of the heavens showing the sun, moon, the known planets, the zodiac, etc. The Elizabethan stage, like many of the pageants, was emblematic in its construction in that it placed Man above Hell but below the Heavens. Devils might emerge from trap doors but Gods made a descent from the Heavens. The machinery to facilitate this was in a small cabin on the roof above the Heavens. There was also a flagstaff which sported the emblem of the particular playhouse as a general announcement that a play was about to be performed.

It used to be presumed that one regular feature of the Elizabethan theatre was the inner stage or within. It was supposed to be either a recess in the back wall, under the gallery known as the above, or it was a structure built out from the back wall with its own (front) curtain. No other writer, that we are aware of, has suggested this but it could possibly be thought of as a booth-stage upon a booth-stage, but this might be regarded as a rather unnecessary addition. Evidence from the plays themselves suggests that such an area was indeed frequently called for to serve as a cave, a hermit's cell, a general's tent, Juliet's tomb and so on. It could be used for a dramatic revelation, as when Prospero reveals Ferdinand playing chess with Miranda. Or, in revenge tragedy, for the working of the trick beheadings and dehandings and other such bloodstained horrors. The trouble is that the de Witt drawing shows no such thing as an inner stage at all.

It is our opinion that there was no necessity for the inner stage to have been a regular architectural feature. The players, being professionals, were quite capable of meeting the requirements of playwrights, especially playwrights such as Shakespeare who was also an actor. More puzzling is the gallery with people in it which de Witt shows above the wall of the tiring house, at the back of the stage. There is no indication as to who the people are. They could be actors, musicians or audience. All sorts of theories have been advanced to explain their presence. Were they actors taking part in the performance and 'appearing above'? Were they actors *not* actually appearing in the play but watching a rehearsal? If they were musicians, where are their instruments? (If they were privileged members of the public, how is it that the actors are not facing them?) The most likely explanation is that this gallery was there to meet the requirements of playwrights for an 'above', such as Juliet's balcony or the battlements of Elsinore. Again, it would seem to derive logically from the psychological geometry of the booth stage.

Dr Hotson, in his book *Shakespeare's Wooden O'*, points out, in support of the theory that this was a place for privileged spectators, that the gallery behind the stage appears to be continuous with the galleries around the auditorium. This and other arguments make for interesting reading but do not seem to detract from the generally agreed theories.

The public playhouses, as distinct from the Court and private playhouses, did not use painted scenery as a general rule. On the other hand, the idea that there was simply a location board, a sort of placard which announced where the action was supposed to take place is probably fallacious. If one can imagine the hubbub caused by those members of the audience who *could* read, reading the sign to those, in the great majority, who could not, then no further argument on this point is needed.

The actors' costumes were magnificent and part of the capital investment of the company, or (in the case of Henslowe's companies) the impresario himself and lovingly catalogued by him. Sometimes they were the property of individual players. In any case they must have made a grand display and thus proved the old adage that actors *are* scenery. The Shakespearian actor might well have played a Roman Emperor in costume that, for him, would be modern dress but, when we remember the magnificence of aristocratic Renaissance costume, we can scarcely be critical of a lack of verisimilitude. More than that, similitude would have meant little to the average spectator and indeed cut across the symbolic value of the costume which was contemporary to them. They tended to see Julius Casear as a Renaissance prince in a Renaissance universe.

Philip Henslowe's diary lists costumes specially designed for other emblematic characters, such as deities, ghosts, demons, animals ('exit pursued by a bear'), friars, popes, emperors and most other characters that have symbolic value within the accepted world picture. With all this to please the eye and to suggest trains of thought, together with the nobility and humour of the language there could have been, given the skill of the actors, enough entertainment on the stage to make painted scenery unnecessary, even if it had been at all practicable. (In fact, as the nineteenth century producers were to discover, to try to put a series of short Elizabethan scenes into a series of individual, elaborately realistic box-sets is virtually impossible without destroying the time-flow of the play.)

THE ACTORS

Actors, then as now, came from all walks of life by the normal process of talent finding its own level but it seems likely that the apprentices would be drawn from the new grammar schools. They would have studied Latin and what was called 'rhetoric'. The ability to speak eloquently and effectively is a skill the actor shares with the statesman and so it was deemed necessary for boys who hoped to grow up as statesmen to acquire the skills of the actor while still at school. We shall see later how this kind of teaching influenced the development of the child companies, in the private theatres.

One early book on this subject, Sir Thomas Overbury's *New and Choice Character of Several Authors,* in a chapter entitled 'An Excellent Actor' says 'Whatsoever is commendable to the Great Orators most exquisitely perfect in him, for by a full and significant action of body he charms our attention. Richard Flecknoe in 1564, in his *Short Discourse of the English Stage,* said of Richard Burbage that he had all the parts of an excellent orator ('animating his words with speaking and speech with action'). It may well be that the style of playing used by Richard Burbage, Edward Alleyn and their colleagues was totally different from that of actors today. Also, it may be that Shakespeare's actors off the stage spoke very differently from the declamatory style they used while acting. Certainly, the highly stylized gestures used to illustrate and punctuate the flow of an oration would fit well to the speaking of iambic verse and assist the actor to project both sense and feeling to a large audience.

THE MASQUE

New forms of dramatic entertainment never appear suddenly. They always evolve and frequently grow up from more than one root.

This is true of the masque. Sometimes we see it incorporated into a play, as Shakespeare contrived to do in *The Tempest* and *All's Well That Ends Well,* but it was most often presented as a full evening's entertainment. The content was usually derived from mythology but frequently with a pastoral flavour. *The Tempest* masque is, in many ways, typical. Classical goddesses such as Juno and Ceres appear, but there are also dances for rustic swains and damsels. This form of theatre always had an atmosphere of contrivance and artificiality. It is impossible to imagine the gods and goddesses that appear as ever being concerned with anything as serious as Greek tragedy and it is equally impossible to imagine those dancing rustic swains and damsels as ever using their scythes and hayrakes in good sweaty earnest. *The Tempest* masque is also

Early seventeenth-century court masque. Note the royal 'state' or throne in the best viewing position and the flying machine for the gods

typical within the play in that Prospero conjures it up to celebrate his daughter's engagement to Prince Ferdinand.

The rural content of the masque has its origins, according to some historians, in old folk customs. This may be partially true but the presence of goddesses suggests that some learned person must have had a hand in their contrivance. Another and more likely origin may be in the 'disguising'. This is best described as a surprising entertainment or an entertaining surprise. Guests who have been bidden to dinner at one of the large country houses might find themselves waylaid near the house by a motley gang of strangers led by a very remarkable masked personage. After some suggestion of brigandage and holding to ransom, the masked personage would uncover to reveal himself as none other than the host and the ragamuffins around him as his retainers.

Alternatively a similar strange happening might be organized to occur after the evening meal. It was a favourite device for Renaissance monarchs—Henry VIII took part in at least one such event—and one of the functions of the Court jesters, then declining in influence, would have been to invent surprises of this kind.

By the beginning of the sixteenth century, the word disguising had come to mean simply any dramatic entertainment involving dressing up. For centuries it had been the custom for the sovereign of England to go around the kingdom on Royal Progresses, exacting hospitality from their more wealthy subjects. Inevitably, those so honoured would feel obliged to present some sort of dramatic entertainment. This sometimes took the form of the 'interlude' (see page 61) but royalty tended to expect something more elaborate and sustained. Grand tragedy or the more subtle forms of comedy might not be appropriate after a heavy meal. The entertainment had to be visually pleasing but with little, if any, intellectual content. To write such an entertainment called for great skill. Shakespeare only seems to have attempted it on two occasions and perhaps merely to prove that he could do it, but his great rival, Ben Jonson, became the most successful writer of masques not only in his own day but in the entire history of theatre. In 1603 he became Poet Laureate but it cannot be said that his great classical knowlege and skill in writing verse were deployed to any great literary purpose in his masques. The best use for them now is as documentary evidence for the theatre historian. For instance we note that in the *Masque of Beauty* the Queen and her ladies as part of the action were received by an actor impersonating Thamesis, the river god, rather in the manner of a disguising. This reminds us of one aspect of the Court Masque not so far mentioned and best described as amateurism de luxe. At the end of the printed version of the *Masque of Blackness* we find that the Queen and all her ladies actually took part, undertaking the roles of various mythological characters.

THE GREAT DESIGNER: INIGO JONES

However, it is the stage directions that make us pause and think. This direction comes from Jonson's The Masque of Hymen—'Here, the upper part of the scene which was all of clouds and made artificially to swell and ride like the wrack, began to open and, the air clearing, in the top thereof was discovered Juno sitting in a throne supported by two beautiful peacocks...round about her sat the spirits of the air in several colours making music. Above her the region of fire with a continual motion was seen to swirl circularly and Jupiter, standing in the top figuring the heavens brandished his thunder'. The poet asked for these effects knowing full well that they could be achieved. Indeed it is very likely that they had been suggested to the poet by his designer, the famous Inigo Jones.

There had been a royal tradition of spending large sums of money on Court entertainment. When Henry VIII introduced the masque from Italy in about 1512 he was prepared to spend about £500 of Tudor money on it, for a Twelfth Night entertainment. By Jonson's time over £4,000 (Jacobean money) was set aside to pay for masques. There is an old show-business axiom that says 'Beware of spending money on special effects that may not work'. With Jonson and Jones the effects seem to have worked every time. Jonson wrote thirteen masques and collaborated with Jones on nine. To these Jones brought his skill as architect and artist and the knowlege he had gained on the Continent, particularly in Italy where he studied the works of Vitruvius (see Chapter 8). It is to Jones that the English owe the picture stage framed by the proscenium arch. It must be stressed that the space behind the proscenium arch was originally more for scenery and machinery than it was for actors. Unless they were to be revealed in some breathtaking way, like the characters in the stage directions already quoted, the actors appeared on what would now be called the forestage, in front of the present main curtain line.

More than an adaptor of other people's ideas, Jones was an inventor. It seems to have been his idea to have pieces of scenery (shutters) sliding on and off the stage in full view of the audience by means of grooves at the top and bottom. These have persisted right up to the present day, with perhaps a heyday at the time of the nineteenth-century melodrama. They can still be seen very plainly in some toy theatres modelled on Georgian and Victorian playhouses. Another feature that derived from the work of Jones, his pupils and successors are the backcloth, which was sometimes painted with an ingenious eye-deceiving perspective, designed on scientific principles. This perspective itself could be continued and enhanced by the wings. In front of the backcloth Jones would have large pieces of scenery that were more trolleys than flats, moving on wheels and capable of bearing the weight of several actors arranged in a tableau. For the first time in any English theatre the scenery could be changed. Not only did it change but its changing was part of the entertainment. By using his machina ductilis (the grooves) and his machina versatalis (the turntable) Jones could bring about five major spectacular scene changes in the duration of one fairly short masque.

In many ways Jones, having studied the classic writers, was basing his thinking upon his reading of Palladio, Serlio and Vitruvius (see Chapter 8) and reviving the Greek *deus ex machina* and the device of the *periaktoi*. (Such effects are generally reserved today for musical entertainments, particularly the opposite extremes of grand opera and pantomime.) He also designed an almost infinite number of costumes, usually mainly in romanticized classic style, but he seems to have delighted in the challenge offered by the more grotesque characters with enlarged stomachs or heads and in the creation of animals.

Finally we must not overlook Jones as theatre architect. He designed and supervised the re-building in 1622 of the Banqueting Hall in Whitehall Palace, London, as a 'now masking room'. It was essentially a royal private theatre, with the king's chair on a platform (called a state, hence the term 'seated in state') and arranged so that the perspective effects were perfect when seen from that position. The stage was six feet high (raked to seven feet at the back), 40 feet wide and 28 feet deep. Such a height necessitated a space between the stage and the king's seat on the front row. This was used as a dancing place, which could be approached by ramps from the stage to allows concourse with honoured guests.

, Several different arrangements of front curtains came into use about this time. Sometimes they were worked from the front by the actors, sometimes, as if by magic, from behind by means of pulleys.

Jones and his pupil, Webb, designed other theatres, notably The Cockpit-in-Court, London, in 1633 (see later references).

We have now arrived at the Puritan interregnum, which ended Jones' work for Charles I. It becomes obvious that the process of change from unroofed playhouses, such as The Globe, to roofed playhouses had already begun. It is true that the Globe was a public theatre catering for a large popular audience, and the banqueting hall was very exclusively private. Yet in 1660 public theatres in England came to be much more like the banqueting hall than the Globe. To understand this process we will have to return, in the next chapter, to the theatre of the Italian Renaissance but, in the meantime, we will comment on the private theatre in London in the late sixteenth century.

THE 'PRIVATE' THEATRES

The term private is rather misleading. The general public were not excluded but probably paid more to go in than for a public theatre. The audiences were therefore smaller but more select. The theatres were called private because of differences in the terms of their licences. The best known of these indoor theatres is the Blackfriars which was built in 1576 for the company of boy actors known as the Children of the Chapel, and taken over by James Burbage in 1599 as winter quarters for one of his companies. These theatres cannot be thought of as if they were public theatres that happened to be indoors. Because the audiences were smaller, closer to the actors, more critical and possibly with a higher proportion of women than in the public theatres there was more encouragement for sophisticated writing and more subtle acting. Their style and techniques would approach those of the Court masque. Indeed, some writers and actors worked both at Court and in the City. At the same time, the coarse groundlings were being excluded, mainly by price.

Playhouses such as the Cockpit-in-Court at Whitehall probably resembled the private theatres, especially in their square shape, the use of lighting and, possibly, scenic effects. (Lighting will be mentioned in detail later.)

8
A Roof over their Heads

ITALIAN STYLE

To understand the changes which occurred in English theatres in the late seventeenth century we must return to Italy in the early sixteenth century. In all the arts, the Italian Renaissance was earlier than the English. In about 1520 several Italian writers, notably the statesman and philosopher *Machiavelli (1469-1527)*, were writing plays in imitation of Latin comedies, notably those of Terence. These plays became known as the *Commedia Erudita*, learned comedy, in contrast to the Commedia dell' Arte or popular comedy. (See Chapter 6.)

The Commedia dell 'Arte was originally produced upon mobile booth stages but what sort of stage would be needed for the presentation of the Commedia Erudita? Naturally enough the scholars of the time looked through their collections of re-discovered classics to see if there was anything about stagecraft. There was such a book by *Marcus Vitruvius Pollio* (known as Vitruvius) who lived from about 70 to 15 BC, and whose book on architecture included one volume on theatres which had been discovered in 1414 and printed in Italian in 1531. Not only did it give information about the later Greek and Roman theatres, but it could be used as a text book for those who wished to build theatres in the classic style.

An architect called *Palladio* (originally *di Pietro, 1518-1580*) basing his practice on Vitruvius, developed what was called the Palladian style and published his own book in 1570. This was in turn introduced to England by his pupil, our own Inigo Jones. Palladio's principal contribution to the history of the theatre is the famous Teatro Olimpico at Vicenza, which was completed after his death and opened in 1585 with, inappropriately for a Roman theatre, the Greek tragedy *Oedipus Rex*. Since that date, although it has been regularly visited, sketched, photographed, marvelled at and written about, it has seldom been used for the production of plays. The reasons for this are highly relevant to our study. Nothing could be more different from the booth stage. With certain modifications, some of which are indeed improvements, it is a realization of the Roman theatre as described by Vitruvius. The auditorium is a semi-ellipse rather than a semi-circle. (Palladio's idea for making far better sight-lines). There is a shallow orchestra (Roman style) between the auditorium and the long narrow stage, behind which is the *scaenae frons*. This is highly ornamented with architectural features—pillars, pediments and statues in niches. (All highly magnificent but also highly distracting and also irrelevant to the measured cadences of Sophocles, besides being out of period!) The *scaenae frons* is pierced by a large central arch revealing a cunningly designed perspective. This arch is flanked by two large doors, which also reveal scenes set behind them and at each end of the stage, facing each other, are two lesser doors.

This theatre must forever remain a museum piece. When we remember that the Olimpico is contemporary with Shakespeare's Globe, then it becomes obvious that *great theatre art is more likely to come from the actor than from the architect*. In one respect only could it be said to be an advance on the Globe. It had a roof. If the impresarios of Elizabethan London could have found means to prevent their performances from being 'rained off', they would have been very happy indeed.

There had been moves in this direction in London but mainly in the smaller private theatres such as Inigo Jones and his pupils had built. The Cockpit-in-Court, already mentioned, had a *scaenae frons* modelled on that in the Olimpico, but curved rather than straight. A later plan for the same theatre showed the central arch so enlarged as to resemble the sort of proscenium arch we see in theatres today (although actually very different in function). It had a kind of perspective set behind it and the other architectural features of the Olimpico were, as it were, 'squashed together' on either side of the large central opening.

Once freed from a rigid 'archaeological' approach, architects began to consult with actors and a new pragmatic style began to come into use. The Teatro Farnese at Parma, built by Aleotti in 1618, is an example of theatre in transition, being a dual purpose building with a horseshoe shaped floorspace for non-dramatic entertainment, surrounded by tiered seating but with a stage between the points of the horseshoe. This stage, like the Cockpit-in-Court, had a central arch but this had now been enlarged to almost the entire width of the stage. The top of the arch had been squared off and the stage was markedly deeper than its predecessors. The Teatro Farnese illustrates the problems that arise when what has previously been a court playhouse, such as the London banqueting hall in Whitehall is enlarged to take a larger audience. Sight lines and acoustics become important. So do economics. These problems will occupy us in subsequent chapters.

FRENCH STYLE

One of the greatest enemies of the costumed player has been the weather. The fairground comedian with his booth stage open to the elements prayed for sunny holidays. The theatre manager of today prays for rainy holidays. It is only within the last four hundred years that it has become the rule rather than the exception for playhouses to be roofed over. There were many reasons for this. Some were architectural, not so much in roof-spanning as in warming in winter and in cooling and ventilating in summer. Above all there was the cost of lighting and, before the invention of safe means of illumination, the danger from fire. The professional players were business men who saw no need for such extravagant outlay. But need arose, not suddenly but very surely.

In England, the change from open-air theatre to roofed playhouse began with the growth of the private theatres, continued through the period of the court masque and became complete and virtually irreversible by the Restoration of the Monarchy in 1660. This simple process took place all over Europe. It was not that Charles II came back from France with a foreign kind of theatre and foisted it upon his unwilling subjects. The English had throughout been following the same trends as the French. These trends were complex but it is true to say that as soon as there arose a need for theatres to be equipped with elaborate scenery, then this scenery had to be protected from the elements. Charles had stayed in France during the interregnum and had seen many theatres with elaborate scenery. It is interesting to compare French theatrical history with our own.

The process is remarkably clear from the Middle Ages down to the seventeenth century. One of the lay societies charged with the responsibility for producing mystery plays in Paris was called the Confrèrie de la Passion. It had been founded in 1402 and persisted until 1548, when the mysteries were falling into decline. The Confrèrie were now forbidden to perform sacred mysteries but were given a licence to perform secular mysteries, that is to say any play except a religious one. They had already opened the first theatre in Paris. This was known as the Hotel de Bourgogne, which had a long and honourable history, being associated with Molière (1622-1673), the greatest French actor-playwright, and with the founding of the Comédie Française, the national theatre of France in 1680.

The Hotel de Bourgogne was a roofed theatre, rectangular in shape, with a long narrow auditorium, into which the stage extended. This also extended back to some depth behind the curtain, making a clear distinction between the acting area on the forestage and the scenic area behind. It so happens that a collection of notes and sketches by the stage designers of this theatre from the period 1633 to 1678 have survived. These give clues to the practice of the chief designer, Laurent Mahelot, who worked in the style known as décor simultané. This is very thought-provoking. When we think of a play in which there are several distinctly different scenic locations—a palace, a prison and a sea coast, for instance, we would expect that each of these would be set and 'struck' in turn as required. Yet at the Hotel de Bourgogne it seems that all three were set on different parts of the stage from the beginning and remained there all the time, with the actors presumably moving from one location to another. At first sight this appears strange but only because of our habits of mind. After all, we would not have been surprised to have seen Heaven, Nazareth, Galilee and Hell all standing side by side in a mystery play.

The origins of décor simultané obviously lie in the history of the Confrèrie de la Passion. For all that their name had been changed to

Comediens du Roy they were still thinking in terms of houses or mansions, in the medieval sense. Basically, décor simultané has obvious practical limitations, but were the alternatives the relatively bare Elizabethan stage on the one hand and Inigo Jones' elaborations on the other?

Other questions were beginning to occur about this time. What, for instance, were the connections between the style of the play and the kind of scenery used in presenting it? The answers will continue to occupy us during the following chapters but, for the present, we can make a few general remarks. Jones' approach to design worked well for decorative drama such as the masque and for pantomime or opera—indeed for any kind of production where the machinery and the scenery are themselves part of the entertainment. Looking forward, it does not seem that it will do so well once playwrights begin to ask for an 'illusion of reality', especially when the reality to be shown is a cottage rather than a palace, especially a cottage kitchen, complete with kitchen sink. But this is to go too far ahead. It is still only 1660 and the theatre-loving King Charles is returning to England.

ENGLISH STYLE: RESTORATION

During the period of the Closure theatres did not entirely die out. There were secret performances in London but, generally, knowledge and skill had been lost. The new impresarios had to make a new theatre in new buildings for a new audience. Charles II introduced a system of monopolies which lasted until 1843. This meant that the Crown granted licences to a limited number of managers of public theatres who paid the Crown for the privilege. This licence was known as the Royal Patent. From this stemmed the concept of 'legitimate theatre' and the granting of the title Theatre Royal which was to be important in subsequent years.

The old playhouses had been closed for eighteen years and were either demolished or converted to other uses. Sir William Davenant and Thomas Killigrew, who were the first two licensees, began by converting tennis courts. (The game referred to is not the modern *lawn* tennis but *real* tennis which was played in a roofed rectangular building.) Molière had done likewise earlier in the century in France. Of the two, Davenant was more immediately successful than Killigrew in judging that public taste would prefer scenic theatre, which was rather like the court masque, though less elaborate.

Sir Christopher Wren was called upon to build theatres in a new style for both impresarios. These included the first Theatre Royal, Drury Lane to be so called, built in 1674. Nobody can be certain what it looked like but All Souls College, Oxford, possesses two drawings by Wren of theatres. One seems to be a project for a round Elizabethan theatre with a roof and a scenic stage but this, presumably, came to nothing. The second would certainly have fitted the Drury Lane site and is usually taken to be the basic plan for the English Restoration theatre.

If we imagine ourselves standing in the middle of the large open rectangular stage and facing the audience, we notice immediately that the pit in front of us is now raked and filled with benches. These are the middle priced seats and closely packed. (Too pricey for the groundlings whose standing space they now occupy). Even the third upper gallery may be beyond the purse of the poor but, as time passes, this part of the house, the gods, will become both cheaper and more influential. The lowest gallery is divided into private boxes, extends round the walls and ends over the sides of the stage to our left and right. The occupants of these *stage boxes* may see the play from an odd angle but tolerate that inconvenience because they themselves are seen by the audience. A new reason for going to the theatre is emerging.

Below these boxes on each side are two doors, through which the actors enter. This stage area with its doors at each end is the *pro-scenium* (that is in front of scene) area. Behind it was the scenic area. The audience saw only a small portion of this. The simple *skena*, which combined dressing room and store, has grown over the years to fill nearly half the building. Yet scenery was still not yet used to create any kind of illusion of reality. Neither did the playwrights expect it to do so. Such scenery as appeared behind the actors might remain static even though the location of the action changed, say from Rhodes to Sicily and back again. It could also change when the location did not. The function of scenery was principally decorative, for the creation of mood.

The stage and scenery were lit by large candles, suspended in circular chandeliers. There were further candles, in brackets, around the front of the galleries. The whole effect must have been dim, flickering and somewhat mysterious but for the general atmosphere of levity and the traders in sweetmeats, oranges and ballads—and the pickpockets and the bawds.

The hundred years from 1660 saw the decline of direct royal patronage and the rise of the actor-manager. There were consequent changes in both shape and style of theatre buildings, in the backstage organization and in the kind of plays performed. Charles II was the last British monarch to have a direct influence on the development of theatre in this country. If Samuel Pepys, the diarist, is to be trusted then Charles was a well-meaning but shallow and pleasure-loving man. He had spent his exile at the court of Louis XIV of France. Louis was a genuine and knowledgeable patron of the theatre and a true friend of Molière, the greatest actor-playwright in Europe at that time. From Louis, Charles had learned how to organize and legislate in theatre matters.

Enter the actress

It was in imitation of what was, by then, a general custom on the Continent that Charles permitted women to appear on the stage and legislated against the return of the boy players 'in the interest of morality'. In the knowledge of Charles and his insatiable womanizing, that last comment may seem ironical but such a very important change cannot be simply passed over with a joke. By not admitting women to the stage, the British had been lagging behind the continentals. The Italian Commedia dell' Arte companies (see Chapter 6) not only had their actresses but actresses as managers as early as the mid-sixteenth century. This was in the *jongleur* tradition, as opposed to the ritual and guild traditions which persisted here.

There had been actresses upon the stage in London before the Protectorate but they were French and were booed and pelted off. The first native English actress recorded as appearing on the English stage played Desdemona in a version of *Othello* on 8 December 1660 at Drury Lane. A special prologue was written to introduce her and an epilogue invited the audience to comment. Although there is no definite evidence, the actress was most probably Margaret Hughes, well known to Samuel Pepys. There followed a period during which both men and women were likely to be seen playing female roles but actresses became accepted very quickly. The actress, on the other hand, was now at liberty to grace—and to enrich—the whole range of English drama, from popular comedy to classic tragedy. Not that Charles and his like-minded, light-minded and, indeed, dirty-minded cronies were fond of tragedy or even of serious comedy. No British national theatre was founded in reply to the founding of the Comédie Française by Louis in 1680. This was the first national theatre in the world. The British could at least have been second, instead of having to wait nearly three hundred years to be among the last.

However, Britain had no Molière. Shakespeare and Jonson were both dead. Typical of this period is *William Wycherley (1640-1715)*, a master of polite obscenity with much skill in plot construction and characterization but one who would never have dared to go as far in social comment as Molière nor to be as scholarly in his satire as Jonson. In fact, while the new theatres were to show, over the years, the talents of many polished and witty writers, there was no doubt that the golden age of English playwriting had died with the closure of the theatres. The age of the Restoration and Georgian playwrights was silver at best.

For this decline the light-mindedness of Charles is partly responsible. His theatre, unlike that of Elizabeth or even of James I, was not expected to provide entertainment containing matter for thought or discussion. Also, he must be blamed in that his theatre legislation was not at all far-sighted although, to be fair, we must say that some of it was protective. There was a Proclamation in 1673 which was designed to prevent persons 'of what quality so ever' from forcing their way into the theatres without paying. He also declared backstage areas out of bounds to the public. This protected not only the actors but the stage crews, now becoming very important because they controlled 'the vast engines by means of which the scenes and machines are moved', and in those days before electrical or even steam power, the engines would have been vast indeed.

The Caroline period was very much one of transition. As we have seen, the new theatres at first seemed to be an attempt at compromise between the Elizabethan playhouse and the French roofed theatre. Scenery, still under the influence of the designers of court masques, seems to exist as a parallel accompaniment to the action rather than an integral part of it. It is in this area that the eighteenth century made very sweeping changes.

The commercial managers

The role of the patentees, or commercial managers, remained simply that of purveyors of entertainment to the Crown, much in the same way as other merchants were purveyors of food, clothes or perfume. They had very little artistic freedom. Of these, Davenant was a survivor from pre-Puritan days, an ex-Poet Laureate, playwright and actor. He was one of those who not only took part in the 'secret theatre' in the dark years, but had enough prestige to get permission to produce publicly towards the end of the Protectorate. He only lived to serve Charles for eight years but, in that time, he founded the Lincoln's Inn Fields theatre (Originally Lisle's Tennis Court—see previous Chapter) in 1661. It was this theatre, with its moveable scenery behind the proscenium arch, which gave him his early advantage over his rival, Killigrew, the founder of Drury Lane. As this rivalry continued, Davenant became successful enough to be about to expand into a second theatre, The Dorset Garden, when he died. Both Lincolns Inn and The Dorset Garden were managed by his widow with the help of *Thomas Betterton (?1635-1710)* the first of the leading actors of the Restoration. In 1682 the two companies were amalgamated at Drury Lane with Betterton as leading actor, first under Killigrew and then, after Killigrew's death in 1683, under Christopher Rich. Betterton and Rich, leading actor and commercial manager, both emerged to fame in the King's declining years, and it was between them and the forces they represented that the battle for the control of English theatre was joined. (It is significant that, after the death of Charles II, the Royal Box was moved from the centre to the side of the auditorium. Since 1685 Royal patronage has not been direct, exclusive nor, indeed, necessary to theatre in Britain).

Christopher Rich was a manager after the pattern of Henslowe (see Chapter 6) or even the decadent late Roman period. That is to say he was a tyrant—mean and, at times, dishonest. Whereas the original licensees had been men of theatre, Rich was a financial speculator merely and one whose sharp practices had led him into lawsuits. For such a man to take over the leading theatre of the kingdom would have been disastrous. Betterton, with other prominent actors, broke away from Drury Lane and re-opened the old Lincoln's Inn Fields Theatre. Thus he became, almost inadvertently, the first actor-manager in the new tradition.

The actor-managers re-asserted the player's right to be the master of his own craft in his own theatre and not subservient to a commercial exploiter. To this end, successful leading actors would accumulate capital in order to 'buy in' to management. They would then use their managerial power to implement an artistic policy. In this way standards were maintained and progress could be made.

Betterton himself went to France to study theatrical effects and introduced them into productions at the Opera House in the Haymarket, now Her Majesty's Theatre, originally built by the architect-playwright *Sir John Vanburgh (1664-1726)*. He also began a vogue, to be followed by other actor-managers, of 'adapting Shakespeare for his own stage and his own times. This practice does not always achieve admirable results but at least it keeps the classics in the repertoire. Typically, again, Betterton married a leading actress. Theatre history is full of examples of this, and actor-managers who found, as it were, 'royal families'.

The actor-managers of Britain, from Betterton's day till the nineteenth century, kept the ultimate control of theatre from being lost by the artists working in it, as happened later in the film industry and, to some extent, in television. Distinguished actors such as Garrick, Irving and many others made up for the lamentable lack of great playwrights. They applied strict disciplines to their companies and so raised artistic standards. All the innovations in theatre and stage design in the eighteenth and nineteenth centuries occurred during the reigns of one or other of the great actor-managers. To say that these men reigned is apposite. In their own theatres, Garrick and his like were absolute monarchs. They deferred to the wishes of their public but were never subservient to it. They gave it what they wished to give it and, most of the time, the public enjoyed it.

Actor-managership was not new. As a basic relationship it was already as old as the art itself but the commercial organization of it allowed it to survive in a commercially competitive age. In many forms, it still survives today. This commercial pressure was a major factor in the process of change in the form of the playhouse.

The Theatre Royal, Drury Lane, as built by Wren, remained under the notorious Christopher Rich who, desiring to increase the money-making capacity of the house, had the stage cut back to increase the size of the pit. He also replaced one proscenium door on each side of the stage by a stage box. This gave the actors less space and limited the possibility for entrance in front of the scenic area. Rich, although unaware of it, was edging his players towards an artistic change. The actors were now four feet further away from their audience. This affected their technique. It was almost as if the player was being guided to play *within* instead of *in front of* the scenic area.

ENGLISH STYLE: GEORGIAN

Although there is a print of Betterton as Hamlet which suggests that the scene in the Queen's chamber might well have been played instage, that is to say, within the scenic area, there is no proof of this. Changes tended to be gradual and the concept of 'realistic settings' was to take a lot of time to be fully realized.

Christopher Rich left Drury Lane in 1709 and soon afterwards died. His son, John Rich, was a successful actor-manager, famous for being the presenter of the *Beggar's Opera* in 1727. In 1732 he built a new Theatre Royal, the ancestor of the present Royal Opera House, on land that had

*Typical interior of provincial Georgian theatre
(based on the Theatre in Richmond, Yorkshire)*

been part of the garden of a convent, hence the Covent Garden. Drury Lane, as enlarged by Rich the elder, had more than two thousand seats at this time. (The first theatre for Killigrew's original company had held a mere seven hundred). The Covent Garden theatre of Rich the younger had 1897 seats, nearly as many as Drury Lane. There were three rows of boxes, a fan-shaped pit and two galleries. Theatre galleries began to increase in size about this time. Rich introduced another new feature—the orchestra pit—which further separated the actor from the audience. On the other hand, much of the entertainment offered was musical even in the patent houses. For the non-patent theatres that were now being built, musical items had to be the staple fare because they were forbidden to present plays.

Licensing Act 1737

This was in obedience to the Theatres Licensing Act of 1737, which had two main intentions. The first was to limit the number of theatres by limiting the licences issued by the Lord Chamberlain. At first, only the true Theatres Royal, or patent houses such as Drury Lane, Covent Garden and the Haymarket, were so licenced. The others blandly continued to provide entertainment under the legal fiction of performing plays and calling them concerts. A relaxation of the law in 1788 virtually abolished the distinction between patent and non-patent theatres. From that time also, it became customary for a large local theatre to take the title Theatre Royal without any patent rights at all.

The other intention of the Act derived from the duties of the Lord Chamberlain as Master of the Revels. This gave him powers of dramatic censorship through the licensing of plays as well as theatres. These powers were used in a variety of ways by successive censors until the office was abolished in 1968.

Eighteenth-century actors

The style of acting in the early eighteenth century appears to have been mainly declamatory. The skill of the actor lay in his vocal effects and his formalized gesture. The great exponent was *James Quin (1693-1766)* who specialized in playing tragedy. The style had honourable origins in the rhetoric of the Elizabethans and the formal training of the Comédie Française, but it would not do for the eighteenth century.

David Garrick (1717-1779) saw this clearly and from the beginning of his career played with a relaxed and apparently natural speech and gesture. He modelled his characterization not on the theories of rhetoric but on close and careful observation of real people. As manager of Drury Lane from 1747 he presented very varied programmes including his own plays and adaptations from Shakespeare and other writers. He is a superb example of the successful player in favourable circumstances. He was the idol of his public, respected and obeyed by his fellow artists (for the most part) and he had friends in all ranks of society, many in politics and the arts.

Under Garrick at Drury Lane was *Philip de Loutherbourg (1714-1812)*, the scenic director. Just as Garrick himself had introduced natural speech for actors, so de Loutherbourg introduced naturalism into scenic conventions.

Scenery now became a more integral part of the play. Scenic designers became very important people in their theatres over the years of this century and the next. So much so that, as we shall see, they became just as well known as the actor-managers with whom they worked. There is a picture of Garrick as King Lear, in 1761, against such scenery as de Loutherbourg might have designed. A stricken tree is seen behind the actor and a broken branch lies at his feet. There is a tree stump slightly instage, whilst a backcloth cleverly painted and lit represents a stormy sky. This setting must have seemed startlingly realistic in its day.

De Loutherbourg was a pioneer in stage lighting. Using patent oil lamps, he lit the scenic area from *behind* and *above* the proscenium arch, thus increasing the effect of the scenery and making the scenic area, in fact, better lit than the apron or forestage itself. He also became famous for his special lighting effects, such as sunlight, moonlight, fire or volcanoes, and for his sound effects of storm, gunfire, and so on. His effects could never have been achieved had the audience been still permitted to litter the front of the stage. In spite of the proclamation of Charles II and the efforts of previous managers, there were still many people who seemed to think that the best place to see the show was from the stage itself. Garrick finally got rid of them and they have never returned since.

Whether because of clearing his stage, or because of his popularity, Garrick had to enlarge his theatre twice. There were minor alterations in 1762, but in 1775 Robert Adam, a famous architect-draughtsman of the period, undertook a period of enlargement. Once again, as at Covent Garden, the stage was cut back, an orchestra pit introduced, but the great expansion was in the gallery. In 1776 Garrick retired. Although Drury Lane was still to play a large part in theatre history we shall leave it, for the moment, in order to consider developments that were taking place elsewhere.

Provincial theatres

Theatres were becoming very popular in the provinces, where the Puritan domination was beginning to fade. Centres of population, large enough to have prosperous and leisured people in sufficient numbers began to have their own theatres. The city of Bath, as might be expected, had a theatre that opened as early as 1750 and received a Royal Patent to be called Theatre Royal in 1768.

The pattern of building was remarkably uniform throughout the kingdom from Yorkshire to Cornwall and this facilitated the touring system, which we shall describe later, as it reached its peak in the nineteenth century.

There was at least one interesting exception which was a sort of halfway house between the Restoration and the Georgian style of building. It was at Kings Lynn and was also unique in that it was built in 1766 inside the already existing medieval Guildhall of St George. A model by Dr Southern still exists.

The basic problem for theatre designers of the period was the conflict between the needs of the actors and the needs of the managers. (This of course, is an eternal problem but it was aggravated as the theatre industry grew bigger in the eighteenth century).

Scenery takes time and skill to make. Therefore it is expensive and may eventually become as important in the theatre as the actors themselves, which, naturally, actors tend to resent. In the seventeenth and eighteenth centuries, the scenery remained behind the actor but was taking more and more space in the theatre. The proscenium (in front of scene) area was sacred to the actor. He wanted this area to be as large as possible to permit free movement but he also wanted to get as close as possible to his audience. If the play was complicated, then he might need more than two doors on the stage to work effective entrances. (*The Double Dealer* by Congreve may well have been played with five doors!). But, as we have seen, the tendency from the Teatro Olimpico onwards was to reduce the number of doors on the stage, first to two on each side and then to only one on each side.

The managers saw a chance here to substitute stage boxes in place of the doors, and when we study plans of the theatres of this period, whether urban or provincial, we notice how the managers are constantly increasing the possible revenues by enlarging galleries and cutting back the stage. The actor is constantly being pushed back out of his proscenium hall into the scenic area itself. Entrances that can no longer be made through the proscenium doors have to be made through the wings. An actor from a city theatre with two pairs of doors to play with may have arrived in a provincial theatre which was smaller and had only one pair of doors. Naturally the actor would have solved his problem by making exits and entrances within the scenic area. This commonsense solution may not appear to be very dramatic but it was to have a marked effect on scenic designs of the future.

The principal playhouses of the provinces were smaller versions of the London Theatres Royal, although cities like Manchester had theatres which rivalled the capital in size and appointments. However, they could not be used all the year round, so it became a general practice to cover the sloping pit with boards to make a dance floor in the off season. This fitted neatly with the line of the boxes, which became sitting-out places. The orchestra would have played from the stage and an atmosphere of luxury was attained, far exceeding that of the local Market Hall or Corn Exchange. It became a practice in later years to build other kinds of dual purpose theatre, including one within living memory in which the pit seating and floor were removed to reveal a swimming bath underneath.

Sheridan and spectacle

To return to London. After Garrick's retirement, Drury Lane was managed by *Sheridan (1751-1816)*. He was Irish born, Harrow educated, a playwright, a member of Parliament, a wit and, for most of his career, near-bankrupt. However, under him the theatre maintained its prestige. When it was damaged by rioters in 1780, it was considered important enough to merit a detachment of Guards to protect it during the night, just like any other royal establishment. Sheridan was a believer in spectacle as a means of attracting the public and being always in need of money, he determined to expand. After rebuilding, the theatre opened again in 1794 and proved itself to be a leviathan. It seated 3611 people in five tiers of boxes and enlarged horseshoe-shaped pit. Above the boxes was the deep circle and above that, again, a large gallery. There were no less than four stage boxes on each side (the view from the topmost ones must have been very limited) and, as we might have expected, a relatively shallow stage with no proscenium doors. This would look like an all-out victory for management against actors but, after some protests, the proscenium doors were brought back. Even so, it was obvious that change was inevitable.

In so large a theatre, it is a wonder that the subtle wit of Sheridan's own plays could have been projected all the way to the back of that high, deep gallery. There was no doubt, however, that Drury Lane had become a theatre equipped for spectacle of all kinds. This tradition has persisted right down to the present day when even Shakespeare, as some critics have pointed out, tends to be produced as if it were a Drury Lane pantomime.

The basic scenic pattern was that of a picture frame made by wings on each side, set in perspective, and borders above, also set in perspective, so that all movements of stage hands were hidden from the audience and the sight lines were limited and preserved.

De Loutherbourg was by now introducing more cut-out wings and flats (like Garrick's fallen tree for *King Lear*). He arranged these cut-out and sometimes perforated flats one behind the other to give the illusion of depth and perspective. He also used gauzes (semi-transparent or translucent curtains) to help his cloud effects. Actors were provided with different levels to work on by the use of ramps and platforms, again masked by cut-out ground rows to maintain the illusion. Illusion was becoming the ultimate aim of stage designers. By now the effects they were achieving were as much an attraction for the public as the plays or the actors. Indeed, some pieces were written with no other end than to exploit the talent of designers. For a production entitled *The Wonders of Derbyshire or Harlequin at the Peak*, de Leutherbourg actually visited the region he was to depict and made copious studies of light and scenery. The final effect must have been rather like a gigantic peepshow with live actors, probably very aware of their supporting role.

With all that wood and canvas and patent oil lighting, the fire risk was great. The architect, Holland, had installed the first iron safety curtain but, nevertheless, in 1809 Drury Lane burnt down. A similar fate had befallen Covent Garden in the previous year when 23 firemen lost their lives and Handel's organ and opera manuscripts were destroyed. After these fires, legislation was tightened up and it became compulsory to raise and lower the safety curtain in front of the audience at every performance.

Some features that we have noted in this chapter have remained with us from the eighteenth century, especially one or two delightful and beautiful theatre buildings. Some of the methods of scenic construction remain, especially the rostrum, the ramp and sometimes wings and borders. Generally, though, eighteenth-century scenic effects are no longer used except to obtain a period atmosphere. The same is true of lighting entirely from within the picture-frame proscenium opening.

Much had happened since the Restoration. Charles Stuart's rowdy courtiers had been tamed and finally ejected from the stage and forbidden to go behind, unless invited. The actor-managers were in charge and ruling wisely. This was the eighteenth century. The keynotes were elegance, wit, moderation, balance. This was the Age of Reason. Why, then, were there iron spikes on the top of the partition of the orchestra pit at Covent Garden? Times were changing, still.

9
The Nineteenth Century

The eighteenth century in Europe effectively ended with the French Revolution in 1789 which, unlike the English Revolution of 1642 and the Russian Revolution of 1917, had little direct effect on the history of theatre. In France the Comédie Française survived and even flourished. British Theatre was affected but not immediately or directly. Government censorship, which had existed in some form or other since the Tudors, was tightened a little, perhaps, but no one was writing propaganda drama as yet. There had been a polarization of opinion into extremes as expressed in the writing of the time. Burke was very much against revolutionary change, while Tom Paine was very much for it.

There was unrest and class mistrust which showed itself in public behaviour that was more than boisterous. Audiences, particularly in London, were never entirely docile. (We would say 'and a good thing too!' A tame audience is an audience that is not interested enough to care.) Our ancestors at the theatre often behaved like the present-day football hooligan. They threw bottles or coins at the stage. Sometimes they started fights amongst themselves, or partisan fights against critics of actors they admired. They were quite capable of invading the stage and smashing the scenery. Hence the spikes protecting the orchestra pit at Covent Garden and other theatres. Just like today, they could sometimes be appeased or silenced by direct appeal or reprimand from a favourite performer or manager. There were occasions, however, when not even a Garrick or a Sheridan could have calmed them.

Such a revolt, by no means the only one in this period, was the Old Price Riots at Covent Garden in 1809. *John Philip Kemble (1757–1823)*, an actor-manager who was 'more respected than loved', had just rebuilt and enlarged his theatre to contain 3,000 seats. This would have been expensive anyway but inflation had made it worse. So he put up the prices. Immediately, there was a protest, with the boxes joining gallery and pit to organize demonstrations with placards, chanting of slogans, ringing of bells, etc, so that the actors were drowned night after night for no less than 67 nights until, at last, Kemble conceded defeat.

SCENIC ILLUSION AND DISILLUSION
To use Dr Southern's terminology, theatre in Europe passed through two

phases in the nineteenth century: 'scenic illusion', followed by 'disillusion'.

As we write, in the late twentieth century, directors are completely free to set their plays in any style and convention they choose and audiences have become used to being offered a wide variety of styles. This was not always so. Audiences used to have rather rigid ideas as to what was 'proper theatre'. However, the wide range of scenic conventions arose because managers and their designers were trying to solve two problems. First, *how much* scenery does an actor need? Second, *what kind* of scenery?

In the first phase (the phase of 'illusion', in the late eighteenth and early nineteenth centuries all over Europe) the answer was 'as much scenery as possible to give as complete an illusion as possible'. De Loutherbourg had used flats (canvas stretched on wooden frames, then painted), rostra and ramps but very little other 'built stuff'. This sounds like slang but it is the technical term for all three-dimensional scenery, including not only rostra but steps, staircases, trees, columns and complete buildings with their own doors and windows. They provide different acting levels, are visibly solid and, sometimes, can be moved with actors *on* them thus facilitating rapid changes.

Of course Inigo Jones had used built stuff but *William Capon (1757—1827)*, scenic director at Drury Lane and later at Covent Garden, saw his built stuff as an opportunity to apply the fruits of his archaeological research. He held that if he was called upon to erect a street scene for, say, *Richard III*, then the fronts of the buildings should be so that Richard himself would have recognized them. John Philip Kemble was another pedant who made reforms in costume design to come into line with Capon's scenic reforms.

Garrick had followed the custom begun by Burbage of playing most of his Shakespeare parts in the dress of his own time. Exceptions were made for classical, that is Greek or Roman, or oriental characters. Under Kemble, and for many years to come, costume designers were expected to research for historical accuracy. The crowning achievement of Kemble's work was the production by J R Planché in 1821 of Shakespeare's *King John* which was intended to be as historically accurate as possible. This set a fashion which lasted for the rest of the century and, indeed, into the next. The fact that it was artistically inappropriate to produce Shakespeare in this archaeological way does not seem to have occurred to the distinguished men who did it. Neither do they seem to have realized that, in terms of theatre arts, such an approach is *un*historical.

This was a time when many changes took place around the stage itself. We have mentioned the limitations of acting space in front of the scenic area and how this had forced the actors to make entrances from the wings. Since the wings were part of a setting that was supposed to be real (eg the battlements of Elsinore or a garden with a box tree) it would break the illusion if the actors entered from the proscenium arch doors. A convention arose that these would be used only when the script called for a door. That, at least, was the intention of designers and managers but both of these groups began to wish to abolish these unvarying pieces of stage furniture.

The early nineteenth-century managers not only wished to abolish the doors but forbade the actors to come out of the gilded picture frame which replaced the old proscenium arch. This process began in Drury Lane in about 1812. Some actors complained about the wasted no-man's-land of forestage which remained empty. Sometimes they trespassed across it in order to get close to their beloved audiences.

By the middle of the century, the forestage was drastically reduced still more, the orchestra pit was moved forward to the new line of the stage and the space thus created *in front* of the pit was filled with yet more seats. This gave rise to a new box-office category—the orchestra stalls. One more large change occurred which affected the very appearance of theatres from the outside. It had become increasingly difficult to dispose of scenery not in immediate use but soon to be required. (eg Tonight's Act 1 scenery to make room for Act 2). Rolling backdrops were likely to crack the expensive paintwork and, in any case, there was an increasing amount of scenery which could not be so treated. The answer to this problem was to 'fly', that is to raise the scenery vertically upwards, in one piece, to a space above the stage. It is obvious that this space must be as high and as wide and as deep as the stage itself. Seen from outside it looks like a tower and, in fact, it is called the fly tower.

The front curtain (which has a complicated history, almost worthy of a book to itself) now became, as it is today, a regular feature of most theatres with its brightly coloured folds suggesting that splendours await within. And what splendours there were!

Charles Kean (1811–1868), son of the truly great actor *Edmund Kean (1787–1833),* had little of his father's acting talent. Instead he elaborated further in the direction of historical built stuff and some painting. In Robert Speaight's book, *Shakespeare on the Stage,* there is a picture of his production of *Henry V.* A first reaction on looking at this scene is disbelief that a stage could be so big even allowing for a little cheating by the artist, who might have been engaged on a publicity job, there is no doubt that the actors, having complained for years of being cramped by scenery, now suddenly have the whole scenic area to play with. The total cast was probably well over a hundred including supers and ballet. (It was fashionable to introduce ballet into Shakespeare in those days.) Two of the characters—Henry and another—are mounted on horses. There are shields and banners hanging from an enormous medieval gateway with turrets and ramparts occupied by members of the cast. The *corps de ballet* is dressed as angels. The many priests wear gold vestments. All round on both sides, clinging to scaffolding so that they make a border to the main picture, are citizens of the time in what, no doubt, was the correct historical costume.

It was said for Charles Kean that if Shakespeare's text indicated that the scene was set in 'another part of the forest' then he would order a hundred extra trees and a dozen or so mossy banks. Not all the effects were quite as vulgar as that described above. Indeed, even his opponents

*Typical interior of late Victorian/Edwardian theatre
(based on the Theatre Royal, Stratford, London)*

gave Kean credit for taste in many of his spectacles. This was because he employed many very skilful artists. One of these was Thomas Grieve, nephew of William Grieve, (1800-1844), the first designer to be called out front to receive applause. Another designer, called Gordon, actually consulted no less a painter than J M W Turner (1755-1851) for the scenes near Dover in King Lear.

William Telbin (1813–1873) and his son William Lewis Talbin (1846–1931) carried the tradition on into the next century designing for yet another of the great actor-managers. This was Henry Irving (1838–1905). One set, for Much Ado About Nothing had a church interior based on an Italian Cathedral with an altar 18 feet high with stained glassed windows behind it, surrounded by pillars 30 feet high and with a canopied roof of crimson plush. We must remember this was only one scene in a whole play containing perhaps twelve such scenes. It says much for Irving as a manager that his stagecrew could set all this in a fifteen-minute interval.

Such speed was exceptional however. There are countless stories of Victorian productions of all sorts of plays where the intervals were at least as long as the play, because of the complication of the scene changes and the sheer weight of the scenery.

STAGE LIGHTING

By now lighting had become very important. De Loutherbourg had based his work on the Italians of the Renaissance who had used reflectors made out of copper basins and had introduced colour into light by putting candles behind stained glass or bottles filled with coloured liquid.

Footlights, that is to say lights at the front of the acting area and set in a row at the edge of the stage, were a seventeenth-century invention, associated with the necessity for the audience to see the legs of dancers.

Lighting was always a major fire hazard. Gas, introduced as early as 1817 was easier to control and became universal by mid-century in London and the provinces. It was Irving who regularized the system of gastaps so that all lights could be controlled by one person from one place, usually near the Stage Manager's position at the side of the stage.

Limelight came in by 1816. This was a process which gave a brilliant white light by heating a piece of lime in an oxyhydrogen flame. It was used mainly for special effects and made spotlighting possible. Actor-managers were very fond of it because such a 'spot' could be so arranged to follow them about wherever they went on the stage.

Electricity was used experimentally in mid-century but did not come into general use until Edison had perfected the incandescent bulb in the 1880s.

Whatever the means of lighting, managers soon discovered that it could be used to create mood and atmosphere as well as simply to illuminate the actors. A general crude rule was to light brightly for comedy and to reduce light for tragedy. Alternatively, important people or parts of the stage could be lit more brightly than the less important. From these rather obvious beginnings a new and complex theory was to evolve.

One of the first designers to use lighting to great effect was *Hawes Craven (1837–1910)*, but he was serving a style of scenic presentation which was becoming absurd. The actor-manager responsible for this reduction to absurdity was *Sir Herbert Beerbohm Tree (1853–1917)*, who was quite capable of having real rabbits running about a stage and trees with real fruit tied on to them. Hawes Craven constructed an entire terraced garden for Tree's *Twelfth Night*. It included topiary trees and a splendid flight of steps which appear to have been introduced merely in order that Malvolio could walk up and down them, sit on them to admire the view, and, eventually, to fall down them. Craven and Tree seemed to have justified all this unnecessary expense on the grounds that they had actually reproduced a real garden, which Craven had seen illustrated in the magazine *Country Life*.

Something had gone very wrong. Critics were arising, including some designers and actor-managers, who were suggesting that perhaps there was too much scenery. Others were saying that there was too much scenery of the wrong kind.

The box set

There had been managers who had refrained from self-indulgence and whose work was actually suggesting a more sensible approach. One of these was *Madame Lucy Vestris (1797–1856)* the deserted wife of the great dancer *Armand Vestris (1788–1825)*. She became a distinguished actress and managed the Olympic Theatre in London. She was noted for her good taste in costume and, even before Kemble and Kean, aimed at historical accuracy. She also pioneered the use of real, rather than fake, properties. Her greatest contribution was the *box-set* in 1832.

This abolished wings and borders and could be used to represent a room. It was built with flats, joined together by a system of lines and cleats which kept the flats tightly together, edge on. They were supported by stage braces. Practical doors and windows could be inserted and the whole was covered with a ceiling cloth. Furniture could be arranged inside it so that the general effect was that of a real room with one wall taken away so that the audience could look in.

In some ways Lucy Vestris was ahead of her time. By the end of the century the box set was to become almost universally used except for opera, ballet and pantomime but, in the early nineteenth century, spectacular productions could not use it. It came into its own when illusionism gave way to realism.

When the box set became the normal thing, something happened to the way people thought about scenery. Anyone who has ever changed a box set knows that, given training and practice, it can be done very quickly but they also know that it cannot be changed in front of an audience *as a spectacular effect*. The original Inigo Jones type of scenery designed for masque and the 'Scène à l'Italienne' arrangement of wings and borders could be changed or (and that was the whole point of it originally)*seem to change itself* in front of the audience. This was to become impossible by the time Irving had his cathedral set, or Tree his formal garden with its flight of steps.

Once again changes were needed. The British stage was about to benefit from a fresh injection of continental ideas. There was a sudden upsurge of radical thinking after 1870 which was to alter many things including the basic concepts of theatre in Europe.

Before proceeding, we would like to call attention to an English writer called *Tom Robertson (1829–1871)*. He is worthy of note in that he wrote plays that were anti-romantic. His characters were ordinary people. His play *Caste* has the thesis that an aristocrat and a gas fitter are equally ordinary people. Such plays, nicknamed 'cup and saucer drama', worked extremely well inside box sets.

As a director, Robertson insisted on real doors with real doorknobs. He had no time for ingenious effects suggesting light and shadow that were brought about simply by the skill of the scenic artist but had no bearing on his plays and their message. He was a realist, therefore he was against illusion.

'AN ACTOR'S LIFE FOR ME'—the touring theatres of the nineteenth century

A legend has grown up around the touring actors of the nineteenth century in England. We tend to picture them as being led by an actor-manager of doubtful talent and shady reputation. His own family, including a nauseating infant prodigy, make up most of the company. The others are either totally inexperienced hopefuls or ageing failures, all of them tied by crooked contracts to the actor-manager, so that not even the clothes they stand up in are theirs but *costume* and, therefore, company property.

This picture owes not a little to Charles Dickens. It has some truth in it but we must not forget that, when young, the writer had tried to become an actor. He auditioned for a well known touring manager and was rejected. Unkind people say that he lampooned the manager, as Mr Vincent Grummles, in the novel *Nicholas Nickleby*.

The facts are that the provincial touring companies in the first half of the century were meeting a growing need for entertainment from the leisured classes and that artisans were coming into the cheaper seats. Equally, these companies were a training ground for talent. Many of the great performers of the middle and later nineteenth century began their careers in the provincial touring companies.

There were three distinct kinds of company. In descending order of wealth and prestige and also, roughly speaking, in talent, they were the provincial Theatre Royal companies, the independent touring circuits and the strollers.

The Theatres Royal were not all necessarily entitled to be so called. Originally a Theatre Royal was one that was licensed by the Lord Chamberlain for the performance of stage plays, under the Act of 1737. In 1843, the monopoly previously held exclusively by Drury Lane and Covent Garden was broken. Licensing powers in the provinces passed to local magistrates who still, ironically enough, could prosecute 'common players' as 'rogues and vagabonds' under a previous Act of Parliament in 1713.

Of the true Theatres Royal, Bristol, Norwich, York, Edinburgh, Bath and Ipswich were among the earliest. Others simply annexed the title without bothering about legal procedure. Their buildings were smaller imitations of the two London patent theatres, though they lacked space and resources for grand spectacles. Their companies were bound by strict long-term contracts, again similar to those which bound the London actor. These fixed salary scales and insisted not so much on continual proof of artistic ability as on availability, punctuality and sobriety—at least during rehearsals and performances.

Actors were expected to be willing to play any part called for and junior members of the company were also expected to 'double' walk-ons with smaller parts. Lateness at rehearsal was very heavily fined. Above all, all actors were expected to go on circuit. This entailed touring for a number of weeks around other neighbouring Theatres Royal. For instance, the Norwich circuit included King's Lynn, Colchester, Cambridge, Great Yarmouth, Ipswich and Bury St Edmunds, so the Norwich company would play the same programme in each of the other theatres before returning to Norwich to rehearse a new bill.

Equal to the Royal in talent and with very similar contracts, but with smaller companies and touring smaller theatres, were the private or independent circuits. These were frequently family companies led by actor-impresarios. One of these, the Fisher company, had a circuit which, while it covered much of the same area of East Anglia as the Norwich Theatre Royal circuit, did not attempt to compete with it. There were no Fisher theatres in Norwich, King's Lynn, Ipswich or Bury St Edmunds. They were discreetly disposed through twelve or more smaller market towns and so attracted audiences which never went into the cities.

Similarly, the Butler circuit in Yorkshire avoided York itself but visited Harrogate, Richmond, Ripon, Northallerton and Beverley.

Both Royal and private circuit managements, unlike Mr Crummles', were generally efficient and, perhaps, even kindly in a paternalistic way. Like most Victorian employers, they expected long hours of hard work but, since they owned the theatres in which their companies played, then their actors had reasonable professional security.

Not so the strollers. Even at their best they never owned a theatre to use as a base to tour from. They had to rent premises as they went. Sometimes their venue was literally no more than a barn (hence the expression barnstormer) but more often it would be a market hall, corn exchange or guildhall. These buildings advertised 'fit-up facilities'. This meant there was a stage of sorts with dressing rooms, perhaps, and certainly space to mount scenery, a curtain of sorts and minimum machinery. Renting such accommodation could give rise to an ironical situation. The hall might be administered by a local justice of the peace whose duties included the harrying of rogues and vagabonds. However, a system arose whereby a magistrate would overlook the vagabondage and roguery in order to book a letting and have a chance to see some drama.

Rural England was as hungry for theatre as the towns were. Every centre of population had a performance of some sort at least once or twice a year and the market towns much more often.

Pierce Egan's *The Life of an Actor*, published in 1829, gives a slightly over-written but generally accurate account of life in the touring companies of the period. It makes references to the appalling business of trying to acquire patronage in advance from the local gentry and the horrible possibilities of humiliation on one's own Benefit Night, when all the takings are yours but the theatre is nearly empty.

In spite of the boom in theatre in Egan's time, the private circuits had been disbanded by the middle of the century and their theatres closed. This explains why some old market towns have a Theatre Street but no theatre.

The Theatres Royal were to survive for a long time yet, as homes for a new kind of company, the Stock Repertory Company, in which the actors tended to specialize in certain types of part, tragedian, low comedian, juvenile lead, etc. Also, as still today, the London managers would send out their own companies on tour ('Direct from Drury Lane!')

As for the strollers, as usual when times were bad they suffered most. Times were bad indeed. We began this section with a mention of Dickens. The Britain which he described in his books was a country where most people had little time or money for the arts. It was the time of Gradgrind, the factory owner; it was the time of Oliver Twist, the workhouse orphan. It was the age of the railway; the old continuity was being broken but new links were being forged. The market towns were losing the young people who were going into the cities to look for work. A new audience was gathering in the taverns, waiting for entertainment. A new kind of publican-impresario was opening up what he called the Song and Supper Room. The Industrial Revolution was about to present its own genuinely proletarian art-form — the Music Hall.

Third Interlude

MUSIC HALL

Music hall was a unique manifestation of theatre art which appeared in England in the late nineteenth and early twentieth centuries. It is now dead. Revival and imitations are attempted from time to time. Some of these are sentimental and inaccurate; others are knowledgeable and skilful, but music hall can never be brought back because the circumstances which gave it birth have completely changed.

A contemporary audience, viewing a bedraggled lady with a black eye, coming on carrying a birdcage to sing 'My Old Man said Follow the Van' may well be highly amused. Yet the song, like many others, encapsulates the bitterness of urban working-class life at the turn of the century. To the original singer, Marie Lloyd, and her audience the moonlight flit, to avoid eviction for non-payment of rent, was a simple fact of life. It happened when the husband lost his job—or drank away the rent money. Without the basic tragedy to give it point, the joke becomes meaningless.

In our limited space, we shall take as typical the fortunes of one great manager, *Charles Morton (1819–1904)* and the halls that he owned and managed. The origin of music hall was in the taverns where working-class audiences ate and drank and joined in the choruses of classical and popular songs. Later comedians, jugglers and dancers began to appear. Morton opened a small theatre exclusively for this type of entertainment in what had been a skittle alley at the Canterbury Arms public house in South London in 1848. In 1861 he opened the first theatre to be called a Music Hall. This was the Oxford in Oxford Street, London. It survived until 1926 and perhaps the dates of its birth and death could be taken as the dates of the lifetime of music hall as an art form.

Like most of the halls, the Oxford sometimes presented other kinds of entertainment, such as plays and, in 1921, spectacular revues. Its main fare was the standard variety bill of some twenty acts, mainly comedians supported by singers, jugglers and acrobats. The great solo artists were extraordinarily popular and beloved by their audiences as film stars and pop artists were to be later on. The audience was primarily working-class with a sprinkling of genuine toffs from the nobility and even royalty. The generally raucous and bawdy tone kept the middle classes, especially the women, away.

In terms of social history, the power of the music hall had its origin in the psychology of the industrial proletariat. It was both sentimental and tough; rebellious and patriotic. It is usual to say that music hall was killed by the cinema and radio and the dates of its decline certainly suggest as much. Equally, we would say that it died, as all forms of entertainment die, with the passing of its audience. General education, slum clearance and the experience of the First World War were major factors leading to its decline. It was an interesting spontaneous form of theatre, very much in the tradition of fairground and of the Commedia dell'Arte.

10
Nineteenth-century
—Anti-illusion————————

Richard Wagner (1813–1883) was more than a composer of highly original operas. He was not only his own librettist and producer but a general theatre practitioner of some skill. He held and advocated the very important idea that the arts of theatre are not many but one.

Like many innovators, he began by returning to basic simplicity. Reacting against the over-ornamentation of continental opera houses he built his own theatre in Bayreuth in 1876. This used an eighteenth-century English plan. It had no galleries and no rows of boxes. Instead, it contained the audience within one raked fanshaped auditorium in which every seat faced the same way. (This idea was still regarded as rather modern when it was used in some theatres built in London nearly a hundred years later).

Also, Wagner revived the notion, almost forgotten since the Middle Ages, or even perhaps since the Greeks, that theatre should be concerned with religion and with national myth.

ADOLPH APPIA

To this end he required symbolic settings and late in his own life he appointed a young Swiss designer named *Adolph Appia (1862–1928)*. Appia came too late to persuade Wagner away from illusionistic painted scenery, but was to accept and develop his master's ideas about simplicity, symbolism and unity between the theatre arts. There is no producer or designer working now in Europe or America who has not been directly or indirectly influenced by Appia. His ideas were set out in his book *Die Musik und die Inscenierung* and rested on the two main aspects of his practice.

Firstly, he believed that since an actor is a three dimensional being, then to place an actor against flat scenery, however cleverly painted, merely calls attention to the flatness of the scenery and destroys the very illusion that the painter has created. Instead of flats he, therefore, used large three dimensional constructions, such as ramps, rostra, pillars and platforms. These constructions were not painted to masquerade as churches, palaces or gothic arches. They were quite simply shapes on a grand scale with no realistic details but certain symbolic significance.

His design for *Hamlet* was described by a distinguished actor as a 'dialogue between structure and space'. His setting for *King Lear* in 1926 can be simply described. The whole width of the stage is given to a very simple arrangement of rostra so that there is a clear forward area behind which there is a flight of three wide steps running right across the stage from side to side. At the top of those is a wider space from which five more wide steps rise to a platform at the top. That is all. At first sight such a setting seems *too* simple. It could even be dull. So it would be until the lights came on and the actors appeared.

It is Appia's use of lighting that is his second great contribution to stagecraft. He was one of the first of the great designers to see the possibilities of electric light. Even without the advantages of electricity, even with gas or oil lamps, actors lit on such simple sets as Appia designed have a great advantage over actors on either illusionistic or realistic sets. Quite simply, *they can be seen easily* without anything to distract from them. They can therefore work directly on the imagination of the audience. In short, Appia gave the players back their rightful place in the theatre.

Perhaps our greatest debt to him, however, is for the basic theories behind our work in stage lighting. Before we discuss these, however, we would like to consider a particular lighting problem which was virtually impossible to solve before the invention of the electric lamp. This was the problem of representing a scene out of doors with its diffused and changing light. Illusionism could offer cleverly painted skies with some beautiful cloud effects but inevitably they remained unchanging and motionless.

Appia used electricity to light his settings so that the solidity of the construction was accentuated by the strong contrast between high-light and shadow. Moving the light would move high-light and shadow and so change the mood.

More than this, he applied Wagner's precept that there must be a unity between the various theatre arts. What links are there, Appia must have thought, between music and light? Immediately we think of lighting as an *accompaniment* to the action in the way that music is an accompaniment to dance, then we are ready to formulate ways to achieve such a relationship.

This Appia did. Before his time lighting, in the sense of being used to evoke mood or atmosphere, was both simple and crude. The controls were clumsy to operate and most people merely thought of turning up the lights at the beginning and turning them down at the end.

Nowadays, a director expects to be able to light each play in a different way using a different arrangement of lanterns. He also expects to be able to change his lighting in intensity, angle and colour during the course of the show itself as an accompaniment to the action and as part of the theatrical effect. He may choose to do this symbolically or realistically but, however he does it, the fact that he is able to do it, and the methods he uses to achieve his effects, he owes mainly to Adolph Appia.

Indeed, it is interesting to note that when the old illusionistic trick of having the scenery change itself before the very eyes of the audience finally went out of fashion, then changing of lights unobtrusively took its place.

To return to the problem of making convincing or even acceptable exterior settings, we now see that the solution becomes possible if we use Appia's techniques on an open stage. His kind of setting cannot be easily compromised with wings or borders and certainly not with a backcloth. Yet something must be done to mask the bare brick walls at the back of the stage. This is usually done by means of a *cyclorama*. This differs in actual shape, being curved in some theatres and flat in others but, basically, it is a reflecting surface neutrally coloured and set at the back of the stage. It serves to reflect and diffuse light and can be used to give realistic 'time of day' effects, weather effects, or simply to create mood.

GORDON CRAIG

Edward Gordon Craig (1872–1966) did not meet Appia until 1914, yet Craig, in England, and Appia, in Germany, were working along remarkably similar lines.

Like Appia, Craig designed massive three-dimensional settings based on symbolic rather than realistic principles. He also used electric light to great effect and published several books, of which the most important is *On the Art of the Theatre*. Craig thought that theatre was 'not a place in which to display scenery'. Neither did he think of it as a place 'in which to preach sermons'. Having thus dissociated himself from both the romantic illusionists and the didactic realists he went on to say that theatre was a place in which there could be unfolded 'not only the external beauty of the world but the inner beauty and meaning of life'.

Very seldom was he actually to realize his ideals. This was partly because of the uncomprehending opposition from established managements but it is also true that he lacked the training of a craftsman and therefore was not as practical as Appia. In spite of this, he remains a great theatre artist.

There are stories, for instance, of his clash with Beerbohm Tree who rejected some of his designs as being ridiculous on the ground, that, if built to scale, they would have burst through the roof of the theatre. There is also the tragi-farce of his confrontation with Stanislavski at the Moscow Art Theatre over the designs for *Hamlet*. The Moscow Art then, as now, was dedicated to realism and Craig to symbolism. We wonder why he was ever invited and, equally, why he ever accepted the commission. To Craig *Hamlet* was concerned with one simple central idea, that of the struggle between the spiritual and the material in life. His designs were to reflect this symbolically through their structural simplicity and by contrasting colours. Stanislavski wished to bring in much more psychological detail and strongly disagreed with Craig over the role of Ophelia. The ultimate disagreement seems to have been over the simple but very large screens which Craig used as settings. Stanislavski was unhappy about them and they had an unfortunate tendency to collapse. Yet through the memory of Stanislavski himself, we get glimpses of the screens being used to create a 'semi circular corridor with golden walls, a long narrow cage in which Hamlet passed, solitary and in black, watched by the golden king and golden queen'.

Generally, critics of the time were uncomfortable about the way that Craig's sets seemed to dwarf his actors. This was one scene where they saw that it was right for him to do so. As he grew older he seemed to wish, in fact, to limit his actors. He began to work with marionettes and to work out ideas of the actor as super-marionette in a director-designer's theatre.

His reforms of lighting, like Appia's, were simple yet imaginative. he abolished the footlights in favour of lighting from above used openly, as obvious lighting.

Like Appia, both his example and his theory remain very powerful influences on western directors today, including some who may never have heard his name.

REALISM

The years between 1860 and 1914 saw the building of literally hundreds of theatres in Britain, Europe and USA to meet the needs of growing populations. What is more, these populations were becoming increasingly literate. The English Education Act of 1870 brought about the working-class theatre-goers. Many of these rapidly became sufficiently aware to join with those middle-class critics who were beginning to demand a 'theatre of ideas'.

At the turn of the century *George Bernard Shaw (1856–1950)* was considered to be very unusual in that he was not only a playwright and critic but actually an active socialist politician as well. Nowadays we regard him as typical of his time. He spoke for many who were growing tired of the domination not only of the actor-manager but of the scene painter. Shaw and his friends wished to reinstate the *word* and the *idea* rather than the stage effect as the central and essential part of drama.

Shaw propagandized fervently for *Henrik Ibsen, (1828–1906),* the great Norwegian dramatist because Ibsen always raised interesting controversies by his work. Ibsen was the typical *realist,* at least in his middle period plays. We use the word realist as a technical term. Strangely enough the pictorial artists, including scene painters, from the Renaissance onward might have claimed that they were concerned with realism. They painted so skilfully that their pictures could be *mistaken* for reality but what they had produced was, of course, *illusion.* Furthermore the audience had come to expect illusion and admired it when it was decoratively contrived.

Realism is usually defined as a nineteenth-century movement in which the content of plays was concerned with everyday life and its social problems. The actors were expected to reproduce natural speech (thus excluding the declamatory manner which had crept back in the larger theatres) against scenery faithfully representing recognizable surroundings such as domestic interiors (thus excluding special scenic effects) in the telling of a story within the bounds of probability (thus excluding romantic melodrama).

We have already mentioned Tom Robertson as a pioneer in this direction and we have quoted his demand for real door knobs but, even in Ibsen's time the battle, far from being won, had hardly begun. The actors were not yet prepared. If you had been used to entering up centre, wearing a scarlet cloak and through a grand gothic archway, it was disconcerting to enter by sidling in through an ordinary door into an ordinary room. Furthermore, if you were used to coming down to the footlights to take a bow on your first entrance, it was rather much to be expected to behave as it there were no audience present at all. (Realist theatre didn't have any footlights either).

André Antoine

One great reformer of acting and producing styles was *André Antoine (1858–1943)* who founded the *Théâtre Libre* in Paris in 1887. He was to have a strong influence on the Moscow Art Theatre (see below). He produced the works of Ibsen and other realists for a period of about ten years, teaching his actors how to build their characterizations on observations of real people. He also taught his designers how to reproduce on the stage, for example, a slum bedroom, down to the last piece of peeling wallpaper. Contrary to popular melodrama, the *Théâtre Libre* held that 'vice is rewarded and virtue punished'.

This point of view has political overtones which appeal to the Left Wing, in the broadest sense of the words. Liberal, radical, socialist and communist writers and directors generally tended to demand realism from both actors and designers.

The Moscow Art Theatre

The spiritual home of realism in the theatre was Moscow but not because of socialism or even radicalism. In fact realism pre-dates the Revolution by twenty years or more.

The Moscow Art Theatre was founded in 1898 by *Konstantin Stanislavski (1863–1938)* and *V I Nemirovitsh-Danchenko (1839–1943)* both of whom wished to modernize Russian acting by making it more recognizably true to life. They chose as a 'test piece' for their new technique a play written in 1896 by the then relatively unknown *Anton Chekov (1860–1904)*. This was *The Seagull* which had already been tried out in another theatre and had failed because the actors found it incomprehensible. The Moscow Art Theatre produced it in 1898 and made it into a very significant success. (Such a success that a stylized drawing of a seagull became the theatre's trademark.)

For Stanislavski, realism implied the abolition of the star system, type casting, declamatory acting and conventional gesture. He perfected a system for training actors which, itself, was later developed, particularly in America by Lee Strasbeurg, into what was to be known as The Method. Basically, it is a system which while keeping the vigorous speech and movement training which the Russians had derived from the Comédie

Française added a psychological element. The actor was expected to identify completely with the character and so to avoid any appearance of acting. The method is set out in the book *An Actor Prepares*. Critics say that such training is ideal for actors who are going to play parts in plays by Chekov, Gorki and other writers in the realist tradition but fails completely when applied to poetic drama or, indeed, to any play where the element of style is important.

One strength of the system is in the ensemble work. Stanislavski's crowds were not just a collection of rhubarb chanting supers but highly motivated and recognizable individuals who knew and cared about what was going on.

The Moscow Art Theatre remains one of the greatest in the world. At the 1917 Revolution it was protected by Lenin himself and it has continued to contribute much to the art since those days.

REALISM: EUROPE AND THE USA

Between the wars, realism spread through Europe and America, sometimes in association with radical thinking. It was not merely that Stanislavksi's ideas were acceptable to some producers because he was Russian and, therefore, in their eyes a comrade. It was simply that realism is usually the best technique for presenting the harsher facts of life in what we would now call a documentary style. After all, the idea was at least as old as Ibsen.

Notable exponents of this style included the American Federal Theatre who developed about 1935 *Living Newspaper* which was a dramatized and unbiased account of political events in chronological order. The same technique was exploited in Britain by the Left-wing Unity Theatre, a non-commercial organization employing professional actors and funded by Trade Unions and individual supporters. Unity can also claim one of the earliest examples of what could be called technological realism with a production, in about 1937, in which both the kitchen sink and the gas stove on stage were connected to the mains, so that a kettle could be filled with water and come to the boil in time with the dialogue and the action.

The post-war English Stage Society presented plays at the Royal Court that were sometimes nearly as extremely realistic. Writers like Osborne and Wesker were condemned as kitchen sink playwrights and the epithet became transferred from their technique to their social ideas.

We must always bear in mind that realism was never exclusively the medium for political propaganda from either side. In any case there is usually no dividing line between production techniques. Most producers tend to be eclectic, borrowing ideas as they need them. Equally, most actors would admit to having been influenced to some extent by The Method.

The box set, so frequently used by the realists, at least for interior settings, eventually became no more than a convenient way of setting almost any kind of play but especially the pseudo-realism of farce, domestic comedy and detective plays.

No sooner had realism become established than it was challenged. Its critics argued that realism depends upon pretence. However much we may say that we are against illusionism in the theatre we have to admit that it is impossible to be realistic unless both actor and audience accept the rules of a game of pretence. This pretence must never be conscious, and it may be more comfortable to say that we are merely asking everybody concerned to suspend disbelief, but pretend we must or there is no play. Stanislavski himself begins by asking the actor to pretend that he is not an actor but a character, that the stage is not a stage but a room, and that the audience, who must be present, are not really there.

TWENTIETH-CENTURY DEVELOPMENTS

There have been four great theatre artists, all influenced by the Russian Revolution, all of whom began as realists of one kind or another and ended by rejecting realism. Two of these were Russian and two were German. The two Russians were Meyerhold and Ohklopkov. The two Germans were Piscator and Brecht.

V E Meyerhold (1874–1943) was a foundation member of the Moscow Art Theatre company in 1898. He rejected the realism of Stanislavski and made a series of brilliant experiments in search of a new revolutionary style of theatre. With the communist poet Mayakovski, he mounted three famous plays which called for symbolic and stylized playing in completely fantastic settings. One of these, *Mystery Bouffe,* opens with the scene in which 'the terrestrial globe is seen, its pole resting on the ice on the floor. Over the whole globe, ropes representing parallels and meridians are interlaced like the uprights and rungs of ladders.' Over this globe, supported by two gigantic walruses, various characters clamber up and down the ropes. Most of them have not personal names but are simply typified as 'a German', 'a priest', 'an Eskimo hunter' and so on. The cast list runs into hundreds and there are six main changes of scene, including 'Hell', "Paradise' and 'The Promised Land'.

Opera Bouffe is the name given to a certain kind of comic opera. This play is certainly comic but is also a mystery play with communism replacing Christianity. It is obvious that, with its allegory and symbolism, the play cannot be worked realistically. Incidentally, it would be equally impossible to apply Stanislavski's psychological realism to the Christian mystery plays.

Meyerhold solved the problems of setting such a play by breaking out of the conventions altogether and by simplifying each scene to the absolute minimum that would give the audience enough data to fill in the rest of the details from their own imaginations. For this opening scene, for instance, he had a giant sphere and the ropes asked for, and very little else except for some clever lighting.

His treatment of actors was based more on Pavlovian than Freudian psychology and like Gordon Craig, the English designer, he developed a theory of bio-technics which led him to regard the actor as a super-marionette, a part of the general scenic effect, intelligent and feeling maybe but always subject to the director's will. This made Meyerhold one of the first exponents of director's theatre as distinct from actor-manager's theatre or playwright's theatre.

Although Western critics appear to agree with the Soviet authorities in condemning him as a mere intellectual theoretician, his productions seem to have been both exciting and entertaining. Under Stalin, realism and classicism were to be the keynote in all the arts in Russia. Meyerhold's work never received the honour it deserved in its own country.

N H Oklopkov (1900–1967) was director at the Realistic Theatre in Moscow from 1932, but under his direction the work was anything but realistic. He aimed to abolish the distinction between acting area and auditorium and thus between actor and audience. In effect he re-designed the theatre interior afresh for each production. Sometimes he had several separate stages simultaneously in use. Or the audience were expected to follow the actions rapidly from stage to stage, much after the fashion of the European medieval rounds. Audiences were not expected to be passive and merely receptive. Sometimes they were deliberately put under stress by not being admitted until the performance had begun. Sometimes they were invited to join in with the actors. The settings were designed so that actors and audience were constantly being forced to mingle. The style is sometimes used today, generally by directors searching for a formula for artistic democracy but it has fairly obvious limitations.

Pogodin's *Aristocrats* is typical of the kind of play produced at the Realistic Theatre. Like *Mystery Bouffe*, it has a large cast and a series of scenes on different locations, but the style is nearer to realism. The play purports to be a documentary drama about the making of the White Sea Canal. Each individual scene—office, workers' compound, the canal itself, is subsidiary to the huge stylized lock gates which open at the end to release the pent-up waters. The waters themselves are represented by clever lighting effects. There are touches in the designs which remind us once more of Gordon Craig. All the characters are dwarfed by the ever-present lock gates, themselves a symbol of the Revolution and its technical progress.

The Russians we have mentioned were serving a Revolution. The Germans were trying to bring about a revolution. The first of these is *Erwin Piscator (1893–1966)*. As a young man, he was an actor but also interested in the new modernist art such as Dada. He joined the German communist party in 1918. In association with the artist George Grosz, he developed a very individual style best described as total theatre.

This utilized techniques Piscator had derived from his detailed study of the history of theatre, added to his knowledge of the new art forms. Each production was a completely original creation. He was the first director to use film and animated cartoon, in back-projection, as part of a play with live actors. The film would comment on the action by showing, for instance, scenes of war behind politicians negotiating at a peace conference. Sometimes animated cartoon would appear to join in the action, as when a soldier faces three enormous caricature heads of the army doctors.

He was happiest in what he called epic theatre. He produced Tolstoy's *War and Peace* and, when exiled to America, he worked on Arthur Miller's *The Crucible*.

Piscator's greatest colleague, *Berthold Brecht (1898–1956),* was also an exponent of Epic Theatre which, for him, implied using the theatre by both actor and audience to bring about changes in society.

Not originally a Marxist, he became so with the rise of Hitler and left Germany in 1933. Although mainly a playwright, he was also a director and a philosopher of theatre. His original contribution is the anti-realist idea of the alienation effect. This is a technique in which the action is frequently interrupted by didactic devices, such as placards lowered from above displaying slogans or statistics; the projection of documentary film; or direct address to the audience in the style of an oration rather than that of a character in a play. The object is to break the mood and to direct the attention of the audience away from the story-line and from any feeling of sympathy, especially with the central character. The story-line is considered to be merely illustrative of the theme under consideration. For instance, in *The Good Woman of Setzuan,* the *story* is the rather tender and pathetic one of a prostitute who tries to be virtuous but is forced to be otherwise. The *theme* is that virtue is impossible under capitalism and that organized religion is neither comfort nor help. Brecht therefore wrote the leading part in such a way as to force the actress to keep breaking down the illusion she herself creates.

Brecht's major contribution to the theatre arts may well be his skilful use of Piscator's total theatre effects and his making of his own company, the Berliner Ensemble, into one of the major twentieth-century instruments with a high standard of professionalism and artistic discipline.

11
Twentieth Century

We now intend to make a brief survey of some typical examples of recent and contemporary theatre buildings and of the ideas which gave rise to them. We shall end the book by noting how the costumed player continues to flourish, no matter what theatre historians or other theoreticians may have to say about him.

We begin our tour with the oldest, that most distinguished veteran now known as the Old Vic, in Waterloo Road, London. It opened in 1618 as The Royal Coburg Theatre to present spectacular entertainment and was famous for its mirror-curtain made of 63 pieces of glass and reflecting the entire auditorium. In its career, the old Vic has been a 'blood tub', selling bad melodrama at pathetically low prices, then a temperance music hall, serving coffee instead of beer. It was then that it received its name of the Victoria Hall. It became a home for opera, the birthplace of the British Royal Ballet and the London home of Shakespeare, under the dominating genius of *Lilian Baylis (1874–1937)* a great manager and a devoted Christian, who is supposed to have prayed to God to send her 'good actors—cheap'. Such was the prestige of the Old Vic that many great actors regarded it as an honour to appear there—cheap.

After a chequered history during which it served as the temporary home of the National Theatre, it is at present (1981) awaiting decisions as to its future use.

As a building, it is neither remarkably beautiful nor original in design. It bears the mark of war-damage and constant alteration and reconstruction. Its success simply proves that artistic achievement depends upon actors and management rather than upon architecture.

We may also note that in the revival of theatre in England in the 1950s, the intellectual and artistic drive came from companies in two very old buildings—the Theatre Royal Stratford, East-London, built in 1884 and the Royal Court Theatre built in 1870. Even so, most changes in theatre buildings in Britain, Europe and America have come about because people who wished to make a fresh start artistically have found themselves inhibited by their existing buildings and, therefore, needed to make radical changes.

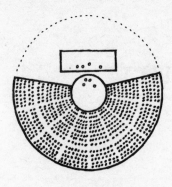

Ancient Greek

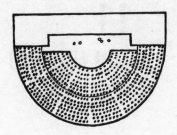

Roman

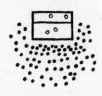

Booth type

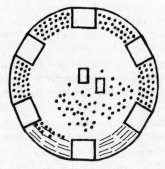

Medieval booths/scaffolds on mound around a central acting space

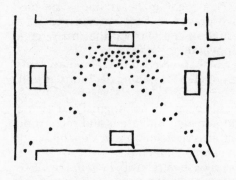

Medieval scaffolds in a market square

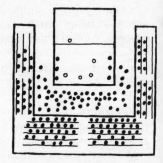

The developed booth — the Elizabethan playhouse

Historical presentation lay-outs showing typical methods through the centuries. These are given in chronological order but the diagrams are not to a constant scale; they are intended to show audience/actor relationships only

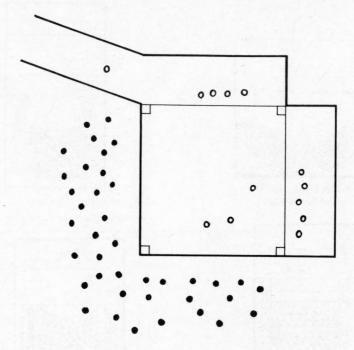

Japanese Noh theatre. Note typical booth stage layout

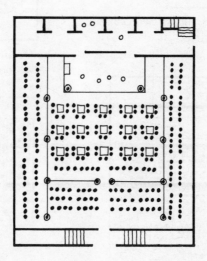

Classical Chinese theatre. Note typical booth stage layout

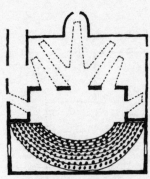

*Sixteenth-century
Italian Renaissance*

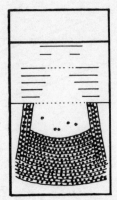

*Mid-seventeenth-century English
Restoration. Note deep forestage*

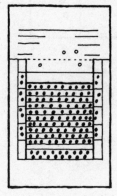

*Eighteenth-century English Georgian.
Note shallow forestage*

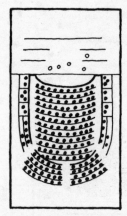

*Nineteenth-century European.
Note forestage disappears*

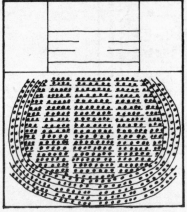

Mid-twentieth-century picture-frame/proscenium

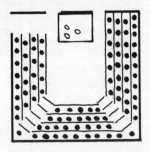

*Scarborough—Stephen Joseph Theatre
—centre stage*

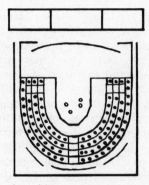

Questors, Ealing—adaptable to proscenium, open stage and centre stage

Olivier—open stage

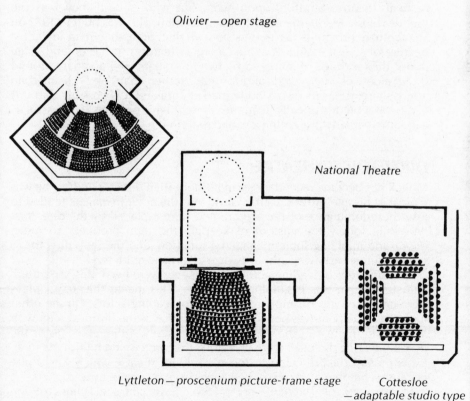

National Theatre

Lyttleton—proscenium picture-frame stage

Cottesloe —adaptable studio type

NEW APPROACHES TO SHAKESPEARE

Sometimes it appears that it might be better to go back to some older kind of theatre. Directors who were tired of the way that the nineteenth-century managers had cluttered Shakespearian productions with illusionistic scenery were beginning to think that the remedy would be to return to the open stage of Shakespeare's own time. These directors also wished to dispense with the mannered delivery of the actor-managers in favour of simpler and more direct speech.

One such reformer was *William Poel (1852–1943)*, founder of the Elizabethan Stage Society. Erratic and unpredictable as a producer and manager, he nevertheless discovered some outstanding talent and was a direct influence on two other producer-managers of some note.

One of these was *Harley Granville-Barker (1877–1946)* who was one of the first actor-managers to acquire a real reputation as a scholar. His books still appear on university reading lists. The other was *Nugent Monck (1877–1958)* who occasionally produced at the Shakespeare Festival Theatre, Stratford-upon-Avon, but who is best known as the founder of the Maddermarket Theatre, Norwich. This was built in 1921 on Elizabethan principles as understood at that time, but it is in fact a mixture of styles, including some Georgian features. It has an end-stage rather than a thrust, dominated by two tall pillars, and a gallery around three sides of the raked auditorium. Rather than any Elizabethan atmosphere, it has its own Maddermarket aura and it is possible that if it had been more historically accurate it might have been less successful as a theatre regularly presenting a varied repertoire.

DIRECTOR'S THEATRE

Monck has become legendary as an authoritarian director. In this, he was typical of his age. After the First World War the actor-managers tended to lose their dominance of the theatre and were replaced by the *directors*. (We shall follow the custom of keeping the term producer to mean impresario implying some managerial function, and the term director to suggest someone having authority over all artistic matters.)

The functions of leading actor and manager were becoming separated. The star system was beginning to decline. This meant that fewer plays were being produced simply as vehicles for leading actors. On the other hand, management was becoming the province of the business man with little or no interest in the theatre. Unfortunately, although some of the new pioneering directors were ex-actors, they were seldom business men. Experimental theatre came to mean bankrupt theatre which was a pity because a number of excellent new ideas were being put forward.

In the work of *Terence Gray (1895-)* we can see echoes of the thinking of Craig, Appia, Meyerhold and Okhlopkov, plus some original additions from Gray himself. These ideas were worked out at Cambridge in what had been called the Theatre Royal, Barnwell which Gray took over in 1926 and re-named the Cambridge Festival Theatre. He held strong opinions about most theatrical matters, major and minor and, for seven years until 1933, he tried to put them into practice.

He began, like Craig and Appia, by abolishing the proscenium and the footlights. Like them, he used large three-dimensional settings but, unlike them, he did not completely re-design for each new production. Instead he had made a number of units, such as screens, rostra and cubes which were to be re-arranged for each production. The rather beautiful and comfortable Regency auditorium remained almost unaltered, with its raked pit and horseshoe gallery, but Gray extended the forestage to make it continuous with the auditorium by a system of steps and platforms. An actor, standing well downstage could have the audience on three sides of him and the idea was that this would make it easier for him to communicate with them. One strength of such an arrangement was that there could be six *extra* entrances onto the forestage and steps, as well as the normal entrance instage.

Gray generally disliked Government and local authorities and campaigned against them for their attitude to the theatre. On the one hand, he claimed that building and safety regulations made costs so prohibitive that only what he called rubbish could make a profit. On the other hand he complained of the lack of any support for drama from such bodies. Less than thirty years later the authorities, not only local but national, began to see Gray's point of view when they themselves came into management, through subsidizing or actually building new theatres.

Gray was also, to some extent, prophetic about the function of dance in theatre. He wrote against what he called 'the tyranny of words' and, under the influence of the Russian Ballet, wished to introduce a larger component of movement into drama. The Russian Ballet at that time was a great influence in English and European theatre because it was such an effective amalgam of music, dance and design.

Gray was very fortunate that he could employ his cousin, Ninette de Valois as choreographer for his productions of Greek tragedy. From the Festival Theatre, she went on to found the Sadler's Wells Ballet which later became the British Royal Ballet.

Other people influenced by Gray included Tyrone Guthrie, to whom we shall refer later, several other theatre practitioners and a large number of unknown Cambridge undergraduates, some of whom no doubt became extremely influential in their lives.

His own plays tend to be heavily symbolic and consciously poetic. He was doctrinaire in insisting upon the complete abolition of props. He argued that it was better to crown a king with a noble gesture than with a pasteboard crown. This may be true but, when the prop is something more mundane, the audience might be distracted into mere guessing games. ('What's he doing now?' 'Stirring a cup of tea, I think.' 'Oh!')

Gray's work, like Craig's was valuable less for its proven artistic success than for the actual act of experiment itself and the controversy it started. Above all there were directors influenced by Gray, such as *Norman Marshall (1901-1980)* whose book, *The Other Theatre,* gives useful information about the non-commercial theatre of the time. Marshall himself later became director at the Gate Theatre, London, and was one of the first theatre directors to work in television drama.

In the period just before the Second World War the commercial theatres remained, for the most part, unadventurous and uninspired. Non-commercial theatre, the political theatre and the growing amateur movement were experimenting in all directions, especially in attempting to break down the barriers between actor and audience. Consciously or unconsciously, they were trying to bring back the element of shared ritual into European and American drama. (We must remember that shared ritual had never been lost in the East nor in Africa).

Sometimes, a practical man of theatre brought about a startling change simply by attempting to solve a practical problem. One of these was *Sir Tyrone Guthrie (1900–1971)* who took over direction at the Cambridge Festival Theatre during Gray's absence in 1929 and 1930. He was later a director for the Old Vic and the National Theatre and was also invited to Germany, Israel, Finland, USA and Canada.

In 1948, because of his known skill in directing crowd scenes, he was asked to produce *The Three Estates*, a rumbustious satire by *Sir David Lindsay (1490–1555)* for the Edinburgh Festival in the General Assembly Hall of the Church of Scotland itself. There were no theatrical facilities, so Guthrie created a very long and relatively narrow stage which thrust into the audience. To avoid his actors staying too long with their backs to the audience and obscuring vision, he kept them constantly moving in brightly coloured costumes. In trying to do without the proscenium arch or picture frame, Guthrie had found that neither was really necessary.

He also found that the deep thrust made it possible for more people to be close to the action than with the usual proscenium setting. (Stephen Joseph goes into the mathematics of this in his book *Theatre in the Round,* see opposite.) It is axiomatic that audiences expect to be able to see and hear in comfort. The basic problem for the theatre designer is how many and in what seating arrangement?

STRATFORD, ONTARIO

In the early 1930s some citizens of Stratford, Ontario, Canada, wishing their city to have its own Shakespeare Memorial Theatre, approached *Tania Moiseiwitsch (1914—)* and Guthrie to design a theatre and to direct in it. There were two such theatres. The first, in 1953, was inside an enormous tent; the second, permanent building opened in 1957 and succeeded in seating over 2000 people so that nobody in the audience was more than 65 feet from the stage.

This was achieved by referring back to Greek design and making the auditorium more-than-semi-circular so that the audience were on three sides of the stage. This was raised and connected to the auditorium by low, broad steps. It is five-sided and has a raised acting area on pillars in the centre. Behind the stage there is a symmetrical arrangement of staircases leading to various entrances on different levels.

The theatre has been successful in attracting near capacity audiences from a wide area but this is as much because of its uniqueness as the only Shakespeare Festival Theatre for many miles as because of its architectural merits. In fact, while it remains the prototype from which other open stage theatres have been developed, it has disadvantages. The 'Greek' auditorium should have been more strictly semi-circular. The stage-structure blocks visibility from the extreme ends. The theatre is too large for its acoustic properties and also its size works against subtle acting.

After consultation with Guthrie, the Chichester Festival Theatre was built in 1962. This seats 1360 people around an open stage within an area of less than 180 degrees. There are two side galleries above the raked auditorium and no seat is more than 60 feet from the stage. This is similar to the Ontario stage but slightly simpler in construction. Like Stratford, Ontario, the Chichester theatre works as a professional theatre for a limited season only.

Critics say that the acoustics are still imperfect and that sight lines are not uniformly good. It is also said that there are problems in lighting, with a tendency to 'spill' into the audience. One cause of these difficulties may well be that the house is still a little too big. As we shall see, theatre-in-the-round can have lighting and acoustic problems but seems to be able to overcome them. Again, some actors have been reported as saying that they feel uncomfortable not only at Chichester but on any open stage. They feel vulnerable without a reasonably solid set behind and with an audience pressing close from three sides.

It might be thought that the open stage theatres could be limited in repertoire. They have obvious advantages for the grand classics such as Greek or Shakespearian tragedy and possibly Brecht, or Ibsen's *Peer Gynt*. And all these have in fact been presented at Chichester. Yet the greatest success of the first season was Chekov's *Uncle Vanya*. It had always been thought that a realistic setting was essential for Chekov's plays. Had not the Moscow Art Theatre itself so prescribed? One conclusion we can draw from this is that Chekov's early failure with this play may well have been not so much to do with the fact that he had been given the wrong kind of scenery as that he had been given the wrong kind of actors and a bad director.

THEATRE-IN-THE-ROUND

If the drama is strong enough it can work without scenery. The weaker it is the more scenery it needs. This truth was known many years ago to actors working on their simple booth stages in the markets and fairgrounds. It is very likely that *Uncle Vanya* was the great success of the first Chichester season because it was so very well acted. Perhaps the closeness of the audience helped to bring out the best in the actors.

The ultimate in open staging is theatre-in-the-round. The really brilliant magician is he who can invite his audience to come quite close

The planners of the British National Theatre chose not to have one large adaptable theatre but, instead, to have three theatres on one site, sharing common services. These are the large Olivier with its open stage, the Lyttleton with its adjustable proscenium, and the small adaptable Cottesloe for experimental work. The National Theatre complex is situated pleasantly on the South Bank of the Thames adjacent to a concert hall, an art gallery and the National Film Theatre. It has bars, restaurants, a book shop and lounging areas. It also provides its own casual entertainment from performers who appear in the foyer to sing, play or dance. In many ways, it fulfils its purpose admirably in spite of its enormous costs and administrative problems.

Finally, in this parade, comes the giant. This is the Barbican complex in the City of London itself. It is being built as we write (1981) at a cost of £106 million and is due to open in 1982. It will provide a theatre seating 1100 for the Royal Shakespeare Company and a smaller studio theatre. There will be a concert hall seating 2000 for the London Symphony Orchestra; it will also be used for business conferences. There will also be two exhibition halls, three cinemas, an art gallery and a roof garden.

We can imagine the original costumed player emerging from the forests of time and gazing up in some bewilderment. Is this the final fruit of his magic?

Postscript

THE COSTUMED PLAYER IS ALIVE AND WELL

If the megalopolitan theatres at Barbican and South Bank were the end of our story, we should despair. We do not doubt that fine work will come out of them but theatre, like any other art, is in need of constant renewal, which can come only from the young, the amateur, the professional experimenter and those who will take a chance.

Fortunately, British theatre is artistically very healthy. As a result of the expansion in the 1950s of drama and theatre in education and the institution of Government subsidies for the arts, there has arisen a youthful theatre of great diversity and promise.

This fringe theatre takes many forms. Some companies have avowedly political or social aims; others experiment with new techniques; some are for audiences of children or young people; some concentrate on becoming community or neighbourhood theatres.

There are about 150 such companies, all professional, registered in the British Alternative Theatre Directory for 1979. Most of them have a satisfactory standard of professional competence and many of them are brilliant.

None of these companies owns its own permanent theatre. They are strollers in the old sense of the word, carrying with them their resources and their talents—even as we write—into the West End of London itself!

From them will come the theatres of the future which will necessitate adding one more chapter to some future book on the unending history of theatre.

Bibliography

These suggestions for further reading include works of academic standing as well as those intended for the 'general reader'. In some cases books covering many periods of history have been included in the chapter sections as their coverage of the subject matter of that particular chapter is particularly good. The number of books available is vast and we have only included titles which have been found valuable and which, in many cases, contain pictorial evidence which was beyond the scope of this small volume.

General
BURDICK, J. *Theater* Newsweek Books, New York, 1974
FREEDLY, G. & REEVES, J. *A History of the Theatre* Crown, New York, 1941
(now out of print)
LEACROFT, H. & R. *The Theatre* Methuen Outlines Series, 1958
LEACROFT, R. *The Development of the English Playhouse* Eyre Methuen, 1973
MACGOWAN, K. & MELNITZ, W. *Golden Ages of the Theatre* Prentice-Hall, New Jersey, 1959 (now out of print)
NAGLER, A. M. *A Source Book in Theatrical History* Dover, New York, 1952
SELF, D. *Drama and Theatre Arts Course Book* Macmillan, 1981
TIDWORTH, S. *Theatres: an illustrated history* Pall Mall Press, 1973
WILLIAMS, C. J. *Theatres and Audiences* Longman, 1970

Introduction and Chapter I
LAVER, J. *Drama: its Costume and Decor* Studio, 1951
SOUTHERN, R. *The Seven Ages of Theatre* Faber & Faber, 1962
STYAN, J. L. *The Dramatic Experience* Cambridge University Press, 1965

Chapter II
FRAZER, Sir J. G. *The Golden Bough* (Abridged) Macmillan, 1954
GASTER, T. H. *Thespis* Doubleday, New York, 1961
HUNINGHER, B. *The Origin of the Theatre* Hill & Wang, New York, 1951
KENNEDY, D. *England's Dances* Bell, 1949 (now out of print)
KENNEDY, A. & GALLOP, R. *The Traditional Dance* Methuen, 1935 (now out of print)

Chapter III
ARNOTT, P. D. *An Introduction to Greek Theatre* Macmillan, 1961
BICKER, M. *The History of the Greek and Roman Theatre* Princeton University Press, 1961
FAIRMAN, H. W. *The Triumph of Horus* Batsford, 1974
SWADDLING, J. *The Greek Theatre* British Museum Keys to the Past Series, no date
WEBSTER, T. V. L. *Greek Theatre Production* Methuen, 1956

Chapter IV
BOWERS, F. *Japanese Theatre* Hermitage Press, New York, 1957
MACKINTYRE, M. *Spirit of Asia* BBC Publication, 1980
VANIS, KALVODOVA-SIS, *The Chinese Theatre* Spring Books, no date,
(now out of print)

Chapter V
EDWARDS, F.   *Ritual and Drama*   Lutterworth Press, 1976
MIYAJIMA, S.   *The Theatre of Man*   Cleveland Printing Co, Avon, 1977
SOUTHERN, R.   *Mediaeval Theatre in the Round*   Faber & Faber, 1957
TIDDY, R. J. E.   *The Mummers Play*   Clarendon Press, 1923 (now out of print)
WICKHAM, G.   *Early English Stages*   (3 Volumes) Routledge & Kegan Paul, 1966
WICKHAM, G.   *Mediaeval Theatre*   Weidenfeld & Nicholson, 1974
WELSFORD, E.   *The Fool*   Faber & Faber, 1935

Chapter VI
ALLEY, R.   *Peking Opera*   New World Press, Peking 1957 (now out of print)
CHEN, J.   *Chinese Theatre*   Dobson, 1949 (now out of print)
DUCHARTRE, P. L.   *The Italian Comedy*   Dover, New York, 1966
NICOLL, A.   *Masks, Mimes and Miracles*   Harrap, 1931 (now out of print)
NICOLL, A.   *The World of Harlequin*   Cambridge University Press, 1976
SOUTHERN, R.   *The Open Stage*   Faber & Faber, 1953

Chapter VII
BARRY, H.   *The First Public Playhouse*   McGill — Queens University Press, Montreal, 1979
EDWARDS, C.   *London Theatre Guide, 1576-1642*   Burlington Press, Cambridge, 1979
HODGES, W.   *Shakespeare's Theatre*   Oxford University Press, 1964 (now out of print)
HODGES, W.   *The Globe Restored*   Benn, 1953
HODGES, W.   *Shakespeare's Second Globe*   Oxford University Press, 1973
LEACH, R.   *The Elizabethan Theatre*   Harrap's Theatre Workshop Series, 1978
LINNELL, R.   *The Curtain Playhouse*   Curtain Theatre Publications, Syon Point Ltd, 1977
NICOLL, A.   *Stuart Masques and the Renaissance Stage*   Harrap, 1937 (now out of print)
SISSON, C. J.   *The Boar's Head Theatre*   Routledge and Kegan Paul, 1972

Chapter VIII
MOLINARI, C.   *Theatre through the Ages*   Cassell, 1972 (now out of print)
NICOLL, A.   *The Development of the Theatre*   Harrap, 1937
SOUTHERN, R.   *The Georgian Playhouse*   Pleiades, 1948 (now out of print)
SOUTHERN, R.   *Changeable Scenery*   Faber & Faber (now out of print)

Chapter IX
CHESHIRE, D. F.   *Music Hall in Britain*   David & Charles, Newton Abbot, 1974
DISHER, M. W.   *Winkles and Champagne*   Batsford, 1938 (now out of print)
GLASSTONE, V.   *Victorian and Edwardian Theatres*   Thames & Hudson, 1975
GRICE, E.   *Rogues and Vagabonds*   Dalton, Lavenham, 1977
JEROME, J. K.   *On the Stage and Off*   Leadenhall Press, 1891 (now out of print)
SOUTHERN, R.   *The Victorian Theatre*   David and Charles, Newton Abbot, 1970

Chapter X
CARTER, H.   *The New Spirit in the Russian Theatre*   Blom, New York, 1971 (Reprint)
CRAIG, G.   *On the Art of the Theatre*   Heinemann, 1911 (now out of print)
HOUGHTON, N.   *Moscow Rehearsals*   Allen & Unwin, 1938 (now out of print)
HOUGHTON, N.   *Return Engagement*   Putnam, 1962

Chapter XI
BROOK, P.   *The Empty Space*   Macgibbon & Kee, 1968
ELSOM, J. & TOMALIN, N.   *The History of the National Theatre*   Cape, 1978
GRAY, T.   *Dance Drama*   Heffer, Cambridge, 1926 (now out of print)
JOSEPH, S.   *Theatre in the Round*   Barrie and Rockliffe, 1967
JOSEPH, S.   *New Theatre Forms*   Pitman, 1968
MARSHALL, N.   *The Other Theatre*   Lehmann, 1947 (now out of print)

Index

Abydos Passion Play   27
Adam, Robert   95
'Adaptable' theatre   129-30
All Souls' College, Oxford   87
Alleyn, Edward   60, 73, 77
An Actor Prepares   115
Antoine, André   114
Appia, Adolph   110-12, 124, 125
Aristocrats   117

Banqueting Hall, The (Whitehall)   82, 85
Barbican complex, The   130, 131
'Barnstormers'   107-8
Barong dragon, The   21, 40
Baylis, Lilian   119
Bayreuth Theatre   110
Bear-baiting   71, 72
Beckett, Samuel   13
Beggar's Opera, The   91
Berliner Ensemble, The   118
Betterton, Thomas   90, 91
Blackfriars Theatre, The   82
Booth Stages   45, 62-6, 69, 70, 72
Box Set   105-6, 115-6
Brecht, Berthold   118, 127
British Alternative Theatre Directory   131
Brook, Peter   20, 24
Brunelleschi, Filippo   53 (footnote to illustration)
Bull-baiting   72
Burbage, Cuthbert   73
Burbage, James   72, 82
Burbage, Richard   60, 73, 77, 100

Capon, William   100
Cambridge Festival Theatre, The   124-126
Castle of Perseverance   53, 55
Chamberlain's Men, The   73
Charles II, King   86, 87, 88, 89, 90
Chekhov, Anton   114, 115, 127
Chichester Festival Theatre   127

Children of the Chapel, The   82
Chinese dragon, The   20
Chiton   34
Choregus   30
Chorus   34-5
Circuit companies   106-8
Cockpit-in-Court Theatre, The   82, 83, 85
Comedie Francaise   86, 99
Comediens du Roy   87
Comedy, Classical   30, 36-7
Commedia dell'Arte   45, 67-69, 84, 89, 109
Commedia Erudita   84
Confrerie de la Passion   86
Congreve, William   89
Cornish plays   55
Coryphaeus   30
Covent Garden (Theatre Royal)   91, 94, 95, 97, 98, 99, 100
Craig, Edward Gordon   112, 117, 124, 125
Craven, Hawes   105
Crummles, Mr Vincent (from Nicholas Nickelby)   106, 107
Curtain Theatre, The (Shoreditch)   71, 73
Cyclorama   112

Dada (art movement)   117
Davenant, Sir William   87, 90
De Loutherbourg, Philip   95, 97, 100, 104
De Valois, Ninette   125
De Witt, Jacob   71, 74, 75-6
Décor simultané   86-7
Deus ex machina   33
Die Musik und die Inscenierung   110
Dionysus   29, 30, 45
Dionysus, Theatre of (Athens)   31, 39
Dorset Garden Theatre, The (London)   90

Drury Lane (Theatre Royal)   87, 89,
   90, 91, 94, 95, 96-7, 100, 101
Dulwich College 73

Edinburgh Festival, The   126
Ekkyklema   33
Elizabethan playhouse, The   71-83
English Stage Society   115, 124
'Epic theatre'   118
Everyman   53

Fairman, Professor Herbert   26
Festivals, Seasonal   21-22, 23
Flecknoe, Richard   77
'Flexible theatre' 128
'Flower walk'   44
'Fly tower'   101
Fool's Plough   22
Footlights   104, 114
Fortune Theatre, The (Cripplegate)
   71, 73

Gamehouses   72, 74
Garrick, David   68, 91, 94-5, 96,
   100
Gate Theatre, The (London)   126
Globe Theatre, The (Bankside)   70,
   71, 73, 82, 85
Grammar Schools   59
Granville-Barker, Harley   124
Gray, Terence   124-6
Grieve, William   104
Guildhall of St George (Kings Lynn)
   96
Guilds   57-60
Guthrie, Sir Tyrone   125, 126, 127

Hamlet   112-3
Hanamichi   44
Harlequin   67, 68
Haymarket Theatre, The   94
Henry V   70, 101
Henry VII, King   61
Henry VIII, King   72, 80, 81
Henslowe, Philip   76
Henslowe, Richard   73, 76
Her Majesty's Theatre   91
Herodotus   25

Heywood, John   61
Hobby-horse   21, 23
Holland, Henry   97
Hollar, Werzel   71
Hotel de Bourgogne (Paris)   86
Hope Theatre, The (Bankside)   71,
   73, 74
Horus   26-7
Hotson, Leslie   76
Hughes, Glen   128
Hughes, Margaret   89

Ibsen, Henrik   113, 127
Interludes   61, 80
Irving, Sir Henry   91, 104

Jester, The   50
Jones, Inigo   59, 81-2, 84, 85, 87,
   100, 105
Jones, Margo   128
Jongleurs   49, 59, 89
Jonson, Ben   59, 73, 80, 81
Joseph, Stephen   126, 128

Kathakali dancers   40
Kean, Charles   101, 104
Kean, Edmund   101
Kemble, John Philip   99, 100
Kemp, William   68
Killigrew, Thomas   87, 90, 94
King Lear   95, 104, 111
'Kitchen Sink' drama   115
Kothurnus   34

Lazzi   68
'Legitimate' theatre   87
Licensing Act, 1737   94
Lighting, Stage   104-5, 111, 112
Limelight   104
Lincoln's Inn Fields Theatre   90
Liturgical plays   53
'Living Newspaper'   115
Lloyd, Marie   109
Logeion   32
Lord Chamberlain, The   94
Lostwithiel   55
Louis XIV of France, King   88, 89
Loutherbourg, Philip de   *See* De
   Loutherbourg

Machiavelli, Niccolo 84
Machina ductilis 81
Machina versatilis 81
'Machinery for Paradise' 53
(*footnote for illustration*)
Maddermarket Theatre, The
(Norwich) 124
Mahabharata, The 38
Mahelot, Laurent 86
Managers, Theatrical 90-91
Mansions (Medieval) 56
Marshall, Norman 125-6
Marshfield Mummers 22, 56
*Martyrdom of St Apollonia,
The* 56
Masks 13, 14, 16, 20, 21, 29, 30, 31,
34, 67
Masque (from *The Tempest*) 77,
80
Masque of Beauty, The 80
Masque of Blackness, The 80
Masque of Hymen, The 81
Masques 59, 77, 80, 81, 83
Master of Ceremonies 55
Master of the Revels 94
May Fair Theatre, The 128, 129
Mehinacu tribe 19-20
'Method, The' 114-5
Meyerhold, Vsevolod 116-7, 124
Ming Huang, Emperor 44
Miracle plays 53, 57, 59, 60
Moiseiwitsch, Tanya 126
Moliere, Jean-Baptiste 86, 87
Monck, Nugent 124
Morality plays 53, 60
Morton, Charles 109
Moscow Art Theatre 112, 114-5,
116, 127
Much Ado About Nothing 104
Music Halls 109
Mystery Bouffe 116, 117
Mystery plays 53, 57, 58, 59, 60,
86, 116

National Theatre, The 71, 119,
126, 130, 131
Nemirovich-Danchenko, Vladimir
114

*New and Choice Character of
Several Authors* 77
Nicholas Nickleby 106
Noh theatre 41, 44

Oedipus Rex 84
Okhlopkov, Nikolai Pavlovich
117, 124
'Old Price Riots' 99
Old Vic, The 119, 126
Olympic Theatre, The (London)
105
On the Art of the Theatre 112
Onkos 34
Opera Bouffe 116
Opera House, The (Haymarket)
See Her Majesty's Theatre
Orchestra 31, 32
Osiris Passion Play 27
Othello 89
Other Theatre, The 125
Overbury, Sir Thomas 77
Oxford Music Hall, The (London)
109

Padstow 21
Palladio, Andrea 82, 84
Parados 32, 36
Paraskenia 32
Penthouse Theatre, The
(Washington) 128
Pepys, Samuel 88, 89
Periaktoi 33
Phylax 33, 66-7
Piscator, Erwin 117-8
Planché, James Robinson 100
Playbox Theatre, The (Pasadena)
128
Poel, William 124
Pogodin, Nikolai 117
Pompey's playhouse 35
Proscaenium 36
Proscenium 88, 96
Punch (*Polchinello*) 68
Puppets 68
Proskenion 33

Quem Queraetis 50, 51

Questors Theatre, The (Ealing) 128, 129
Quin, James 94

Ramayana, The 38, 39-40
Realism 113-4
Realistic Theatre, The (Moscow) 117
Red Bull Theatre, The (Clerkenwell) 71
Religious drama, Medieval European 49-60
Religious festivals, Early Eastern 38-46
Religious festivals, Early Western 25-37
Revels Office, The 60
Rich, Christopher 90, 91, 94
Rich, John
Rituals 17, 19-21, 23-4, 25, 27, 28, 29-30, 47-8, 49
Robertson, Tom 106, 114
Rose Theatre, The (Bankside) 71, 73
Royal Ballet, The 125
Royal Coburg Theatre, The See The Old Vic
Royal Court Theatre, The 115, 119
Royal Opera House, The 91
Royal Patent, The 87
Royal Shakespeare Company, The 130
Russian Ballet, The 125

Sadler's Wells Ballet, The 125
San Felice Church (Florence) 53 (footnote for illustration)
Scaffolds 56
Scaenae frons 36, 84-5
Scene a l'Italienne 106
Seneca, Lucius Annaeus 37
Serlio, Sebastiano 82
Shakespeare, William 57, 60, 77, 80
Shakespeare Memorial Theatre, The (Stratford, Ontario) 126-7
Shakespeare's Wooden 'O' 76
Stage, Shape of the 62-70

Shaw, George Bernard 113
Sheridan, Richard Brinsley 97
Shiva 38
Short Discourse of the English Stage 77
Sight Lines 63, 72, 84
'Sixpenny gallants, The' 74, 75
Skena 32, 33, 64, 88
'Snap' dragon 21
Sophocles 85
Southern, Richard 12, 14, 17, 24, 96, 99
Stanislavski, Konstantin 112, 114-5, 116
Strasberg, Lee 114
'Stylers' 56
Swan Theatre, The (Bankside) 71

Teatro Farnese (Parma) 85
Teatro Olimpico (Vicenza) 84, 85
Telbin, William 104
Telbin, William Lewis 104
Tennis Court, Lisle's 90
Terence (Publius Terentius Afer) 37, 84
Theatre, The (Scarborough) 128
Theatre, The (Shoreditch) 71, 72, 73
Theatre en Rond (Paris) 128
Theatre-in-the-round 127-129
Theatre in the Round 126
Théâtre Libre (Paris) 114
'Theatre of ideas' 113
Theatre Royal, The (Barnwell) See Cambridge Festival Theatre
Theatre Royal, The (Bath) 95, 107
Theatre Royal, The (Stratford, East London) 119
Theatres Royal, The 87, 107
Thespis 30
Thyromata 32
Three Estates, The 126
'Thrust' stage 126
'Total theatre' 46, 117-8
Tragedy, Classical 30
Traverse Theatre, The (Edinburgh) 128
Tree, Sir Herbert Beerbohm 105, 112

Triumph of Horus, The   26-7
Trois Frères   18
Tropes   50-51
Turner, Joseph Mallord William
   104

Uncle Vanya   127
Unity Theatre, The   115

Valenciennes Passion Play   54, 55,
   57
Vanbrugh, Sir John   91
Vasari, Giorgio   53 (*footnote for
   illustration*)
Vestris, Mme Lucy   105
Victoria Hall, The   *See* The Old Vic
Victoria Theatre, The
   (Stoke-on-Trent)   128, 129
Vitruvius (Pollio), Marcus   81, 82,
   84

Wagner, Richard   110
Wajang-kulit   40-41
Wajang-orang   41
Webster, John   59, 73
Whitehall Palace   *See* Banqueting
   Hall, The
'Wild Men', The   24
Wonders of Derbyshire, The   97
Wren, Sir Christopher   87

Yang   46
Yin   46